Thorns of
Chester Street

Thorns of
Chester Street

Shawn Alex Nemeth

ISBN: 1548798703
ISBN 13: 9781548798703
Library of Congress Control Number: 2017910866
CreateSpace Independent Publishing Platform
North Charleston, South Carolina

A true story.*

*Dedicated to all the children of any age
who survived the prick of the thorn
to relish the beauty of the rose.*

Prologue

—— ❀ ——

REACHING OUT TO pick one of the fragrant roses in front of our house on Chester Street, I screamed out in pain as a thorn drove deep into my young, sensitive skin. I stuck my throbbing finger into my mouth to lick off the trickle of blood, but even when the evidence of my wound was gone, the pain remained.

"Why would something so pretty want to hurt me?" I wondered. *"Maybe it was just an accident,"* I reasoned. And I trusted.

Walking through the dark, tangled garden of my childhood, the pink roses continued to lure me with their fragrance. I was completely distracted by their velvety texture, unprepared for the contradiction hidden in their beautiful deception. Once again, they pierced me, and deeper still. Like a big boy should, I licked my wounds and did my best to forget, but the pain remained.

"Why would something so pretty want to hurt me," I asked myself again. *"Maybe this will be the last time,"* I reasoned again. And kept trusting.

In my nighttime dreams, the roses had faces, and they chased me, trying to stab me with their sword-sized thorns. Each time I struggled and fought until I could wake up and be freed of their torment. In the daylight, their faces were gone, but the pain remained.

"Why would something so pretty want to hurt me?"

I knew the answer: The roses hurt me because I deserved it. The thick, toxic vine wrapped around me, piercing me, leaving me dripping with shame and sealing my agony inside.

S.A.N.

CHAPTER 1

———— ∽ ————

ON A BRIGHT summer Saturday afternoon, my mother and I were walking home from the convenience store located just across the railroad tracks from where we lived in our small Ohio town. Our very old two-story house on Chester Street faced an empty field where I often played. The spacious overgrown field with its discarded railroad ties and colorful rocks created a much-needed barrier between our home and the tracks. Even so, our little house was so close to the tracks that it shook with each passing train. When we first moved there, the engine's screaming whistle warning of its approach would often frighten me to my very core. It's ironic that over time, the vibration of my bedroom windows caused by the rumblings of this iron beast eventually became a source of comfort to me in the sad, lonely nights of my childhood.

As we crossed the busy street in front of the store, Mom and I passed the Free Methodist Church and parsonage. This little white church with its beautifully perched steeple and freshly planted flowers served as a welcome oasis in our tired, rundown neighborhood. Pointing at the church, I looked up at my mother and asked, "Can I start going to church here on Sundays?" Without much hesitation, she gave me her permission—probably thinking that it was just a passing whim or silly notion.

With Christmas-like anticipation, I eagerly woke up early the next morning. It was Sunday! I picked out the best clothes I could find in my closet and got dressed. I walked down the creaking stairs to find Mom and my stepdad in the living room, passed out from their previous night of partying. Numerous empty beer cans and cigarette butts filled the downstairs of the house with a nauseating odor. Unable to wake them and afraid that Mom would change her mind, I immediately started out on my adventure.

I could smell the comforting scent of the flowers near the church and thought of how they reminded me of the ones in my grandmother's garden. I must have arrived there very early because the church was not yet open; however, this small inconvenience didn't deter me from my mission. I sat down on the painted cement steps and waited. What was this lonely seven-year-old boy waiting for? Perhaps more than anything else: *connection*.

Up to that point, the one person in my world with whom I felt a real connection was my mom's mother. A kind, nurturing soul, Grandma taught me about God's love for me. I remember so many times sitting on her lap for what seemed like hours listening to her share from her extensive memory bank of children's songs and nursery rhymes. Could it be that it was the love and connection I experienced in my occasional visits with her that produced this driving force within me to venture out in search of more love, more connection? It definitely gave me a taste of what I was missing. I so desperately wanted to be loved and to feel safe. I wondered whether this God my grandmother spoke of would care for and protect me. My developing mind needed to know!

I didn't sit on those steps too long before the young pastor and his wife arrived. The pastor sported a dark suit, his black hair slicked back with a generous amount of Alberto VO5. His pretty, petite wife wore a blue polka-dot dress with her hair fashioned neatly into a bun. They seemed to be the sweetest people I had ever met as they greeted me with generous smiles and hugs. The pastor looked down at me and kindly asked, "Who is this cute little girl?" I quickly informed him that I was a boy and that my mom preferred my hair long (so typical in the 1970s). This wasn't the first time I had been mistaken for a girl; it had happened several times before, only adding to the torment of my secret attraction to other boys.

The pastor and his wife invited me into the foyer of the church and I found a place to sit in the back of the sanctuary close to the door. I curiously watched the pastor as he made his way to the pulpit to attend to his pre-service activities, while his wife began to arrange the selected song sheets at the piano. I was so drawn to their energy and passion. "How great it would be to have parents like them," I thought. I was quickly ushered back from my parental fantasy by the tender touch of a soft, wrinkled old hand on my shoulder. The lady said her name was Mrs. Lee and she asked me if I would like sit with her during the service. I eagerly accepted her invitation and followed her into a nearby wooden pew. She must have noticed my anxiety and nervousness. I'm sure the scared, neglected, abused boy with long hair must have looked so awkward and out of place, but Mrs. Lee didn't seem to mind. As I sat there next to her, she put her loving arm around me and instantly created a safe place for me. She provided emotional soul food for this affection-starved little boy.

With its growing children's ministry and the pastor's personal visits to my home, the little white church quickly became my refuge. I attended as many as three services a week and eventually became active by assisting on one of the Sunday-morning bus routes, serving refreshments, and knocking on doors. The loving folks at the church taught me that I had worth and value. Through their kindness and generosity,

I began to believe that there were indeed good people in the world and that not everyone wanted to harm and mistreat me.

During the night I would often lie awake, pleading with God through my floods of tears and deep heartache. I begged Him to please send a sweet couple like the pastor and his wife to rescue and adopt me. I fantasized about what these loving parents would look like and how it would feel to be loved and wanted by them. I used my fantasy to soothe and comfort myself.

Then one night while I was lying on the top of my bunk bed, I had an experience that forever changed me.

I had a vision.

I saw myself lifted from the room, as if in some sort of spiritual elevator. On each side of me I could see demonic figures—people who had hurt me—and great darkness was all around. As I continued being lifted higher and higher, the darkness and the demons began to subside. I traveled so high and so out of reach that I could no longer see or feel their existence. An overwhelming light radiated brighter and brighter. For a moment, the light hindered my ability to see anything else. When the elevator stopped and my full sight returned, I found myself bowing before a towering white marble staircase.

As I lifted up my head, I saw Him. I saw Jesus! I couldn't see His face because of the light that surrounded Him, but I knew it was Him. He stood there at the top of the stairs in a long, white flowing robe, looking down at me. As He extended both of His arms down toward me, I instantly felt His loving embrace and a peace flooded over me, a peace such as I had never known. He didn't say a word that I could hear, yet I knew He was speaking so clearly to me. He was declaring

His love for me and assuring me that I was not alone. I wanted to stay there forever!

As quickly as the vision had begun, it ended. I found myself traveling back into my dark existence. With tears still running down my face, I immediately ran downstairs to tell my mother what had happened. She dismissively told me that I had been dreaming and to go back to bed.

My mother's words filled my heart with immense frustration, because I knew without a doubt that I had not been dreaming; I was very much awake.

The next day while I was playing in my room, I heard my mother call out, "Shawn, Grandma is on the phone and wants to talk to you."

I ran downstairs and picked up the phone. "Hi, Grandma!" I answered excitedly.

After we talked for a few minutes, Grandma warmly said, "Sweetheart, your mom told me what you saw last night in your bedroom."

"I saw Jesus, Grandma!"

"I know you did, honey. For some special reason, God has allowed you see something that He doesn't show many people. Not everyone will understand, Shawn, but I don't want you to ever forget what you saw and or let anyone tell you that you didn't."

"Okay, Grandma; I won't," I promised.

In stark contrast to Grandma, my domineering stepfather Jed became very uneasy with my involvement in the church. My interaction with the churchgoers and their continued interest in my welfare posed direct threats to Jed's control over me. This seemed to infuriate him and he took it out on me by continually making fun of me and shaming me. I would often come home from church to find heavy workloads and abusive behavior directed at me. He began to punish me even when he saw me laughing or enjoying myself, taking delight in my sadness. The simplest actions seemed to set him off for no reason. I became so fearful of his erratic behavior that I was constantly on edge, unable to relax in my own home.

I must have inwardly known somehow that my survival depended on my continual interaction with the little white church. The abuse, the manipulation, the shaming—nothing seemed to keep me from my safe place. The force of hatred and darkness that ruled my stepfather Jed was strong, yet my will to survive was stronger.

With her brown pigtails bouncing like streamers in the wind, my half-sister Hailey, six years younger than I, yelled, "Sing it again!"

I loved music, and while singing the hymns and children's songs at my little church, I realized I had a voice. I often practiced songs that I heard on TV and the radio while I walked to and from school, and it wasn't long before I drew a small circle of listeners at recess. Hailey was assuredly my biggest fan while we were young, and would often ask me to sing as we played alone. How, then, could I possibly let my biggest fan down on this particular Friday night when she was asking for more?

After quickly repositioning myself, I suddenly turned around, took a large step forward for dramatic effect, and with great emotion on my face, raised my hairbrush microphone to my mouth to belt out another stellar performance. The small bedroom where we were playing erupted with cheers as Hailey clapped wildly! After taking my bow, I quickly made my exit into the little tent we'd crafted with the faded old sheets I'd pulled off my bed. "I'm coming in, too!" announced Hailey as she pulled back the fabric door flap and playfully climbed over me. We both lay side by side laughing and looking around, proudly admiring our creation.

"Shawn, get your ass out here!" Suddenly hearing the angry voice of my stepfather, I froze. Hailey nervously climbed out first as Jed told her to go downstairs. Before I could stand up, Jed violently grabbed both of my shoulders, lifting me off the floor and putting my face only inches from his. His hot breath sprayed me with the foul stench of cigarettes and whisky as he heatedly asked, "What were you doing to your sister in there?"

"Noo-thh-ing," I stammered.

"What do you mean, nothing!?" he asked, raising his voice in anger.

With tears blinding my eyes, I tensely answered, "We were just play-ing, th-aat's all."

"You better hope that's all, you little fucker, or it will be the last thing you ever do. Do you hear me? I said, do you fuckin' hear me?!"

"Yee-es," I whimpered.

Dropping me to the ground and demolishing our tent with a kick of his boot, he said, "Now take this damn thing down and get your ass downstairs to do the dishes. If I find one spot on those dishes, you will re-wash every dish in this house!"

Afterward, the magnitude of the fear and shock hit me full force. I climbed onto my bed, buried my head in my pillow, and wept.

I spent the rest of that evening re-washing every dish in the house. I'd missed a spot.

From that time on, it was very difficult for me to show any kind of affection toward my little sister; even being told to put my arm around her when taking a picture was incredibly uncomfortable for me. Jed's perverse mind had poisoned me, and the shame of his twisted words clung to me like a greasy dishrag.

Nighttime was so frightening for me in the old gray-shingled two-story house. The house held eight rooms, including an enclosed back porch and a dark, musty, unfinished attic that extended off of the room my sister and I shared. There was a long, narrow enclosed staircase which led upstairs to the two bedrooms. The small storage space under the stairs had been converted into a bathroom. There was no heat upstairs, and a glass of water would freeze solid overnight. During the harsh winter months, we would keep our mattresses propped up on the stairway behind the door and then drag them downstairs every evening to sleep on the floor. Hailey and I would sleep in the dining room while Mom and Jed would sleep in the living room. The open doorway and close proximity made it extremely awkward for me when Mom and Jed were having sex. The placement of my mattress in front of the gas stove unfortunately enabled me to see and hear much more than I wanted.

One Saturday night while I was sleeping on my mattress in the usual spot, I was quickly awakened by a loud commotion coming from the living room. As I lifted up my head to look, I saw Jed's brother Owen hastily climbing off my four-year-old sister, who had fallen asleep on the sofa. Owen had been staying with us while my parents were out partying. They must have seen him on top of her through the front window as they were returning home. As my hysterically crying mother quickly ran over to Hailey to hold her, Jed grabbed Owen, pushing him out the door and screaming that he was going to kill him. Knowing there was nothing I could do, I pulled the covers over my head. It was something I commonly did as a child when I went to bed at night: a child's way of fending off the monsters and feeling safe. Still, what I had witnessed hurt me deeply.

A few months later when I came home from church one Sunday, Owen and Jed were on the front porch laughing as if nothing had ever happened. I never heard anything about the incident again, and my poor little sister was expected to forget about it and interact with her abuser just as I had learned to do.

If Jed's little angel Hailey wasn't safe, what hope did I have?

"I sure hope I don't get Mrs. Stiles for my teacher," said Brad, my friend who lived two houses down from us. "Why? Give me the skinny," I asked. He quickly responded, "'Cause she's really mean, you know. Like, she gives her class lots of homework and makes 'em all sit together with her for lunch. She has 'em use a stupid napkin, learn girly table manners and sing that silly 'Kum-ba-yah' song before they eat. Like, how stupid is that?!" he pondered. "That would be a total bummer," I said. "I hear them singing that stupid song at lunch. Like, I hope I don't get her either!" I remarked.

Brad received his wish, but my summertime fear was realized on the first day of school when I found out I had Mrs. Stiles as my fourth-grade teacher. With her stern, weathered face and long gray hair, she surely did look mean, I thought. My observation appeared to be quite accurate as she told me I had to stay after school for talking during class (a curse that followed me all through school).

I nervously waited along with a few other students to receive my punishment after class. Mrs. Stiles had us assist her with a creative project. She had us trace and color seasonal objects such as autumn leaves, acorns, and sheaves of wheat on large pieces of paper which were blown up by a projector. I felt a sense of pride and accomplishment when I arrived at school the next morning to see our artwork prominently displayed on the wall. Mrs. Stiles, who was only a few years from retiring, knew exactly what she was doing. Instead of shaming us, she taught us how to redirect our behavior by plugging our extra energy into a creative outlet. I was hooked! I became motivated to please her by paying attention and doing well in class. I also volunteered to stay after class as often as I could to help. She was a brilliant teacher who made learning fun. She would often bring several items a week from her extensive Native American jewelry and artifact collection to share with the class. As she passed the items around allowing us to touch and admire them, she would teach us a story-driven lesson that exposed our hungry minds to new ideas and cultures. It didn't take long to turn Brad's judgments into jealousy as I shared with him all the cool stuff about my new class.

Mrs. Stiles was strict and firm, but far from mean. I grew to love and highly respect her. I felt safe within the structure that her class provided to my chaotic world.

As I began to recognize the cries of my black-and-white terrier that Wednesday afternoon while coming home from school, anxiety and fear pushed me forward like a tidal wave. Running as fast as I could to the front of the house, I soon came upon the terrifying scene. Jed, with a cigarette clenched tightly between his lips, was hanging my little dog over the side of the porch with a leather leash wrapped tightly around his neck, his little body shaking violently as he tried desperately to break free and catch a breath. I started screaming and crying, begging Jed to let him go. Removing the cigarette with his free hand, Jed lashed out at me saying, "Get your fucking ass in the house!"

I froze.

"I said, get your ass in the house or you'll be next!"

Jed mercilessly beat and kicked my sweet little dog as I helplessly watched through the screen door.

A year and half later, during the worst Ohio blizzard in years, I begged Jed to let me bring Cleo, my new Doberman, inside to stay warm; he wouldn't allow it. She froze to death while trying to keep her puppies warm.

As an abused child, it was only from our dogs and various other animals that I felt a sense of unconditional love. I plastered the walls of my small bedroom with animal posters, and spent hours reading from a set of *Wild Kingdom* encyclopedias, purchased by my dad. With great excitement, I often talked about wanting to be a veterinarian when I grew up. Undoubtedly aware, Jed knew that when he hurt animals in my presence, he was hurting me. He seemed to take demented pleasure in it.

My mother had traded in the violence of one man for another, and she was no exception to the abuse and sick humiliation of her current husband. I never grew accustomed to the gripping fear of being jolted awake deep in the night by the defenseless screams of my mother. The only thing worse was not being able to do a damn thing to stop them. The shame I felt from not being able to protect my mom and our pets from this heartless man ravaged my confidence and self-esteem like the harsh winter winds ripping into a fragile blade of grass. I felt completely powerless, often blaming myself without mercy.

One Sunday morning, after a long, turbulent night, my little sister and I nervously went downstairs to survey the wreckage of Jed's anger. Our emotionally fragile mother, her face blackened with bruises and running mascara, sat alone on the sofa. All I could hear was the unshielded high-pitched chirp of the sparrows coming in freely through the broken dining room window through which Jed had thrown mom a few hours before. Thank God he was gone! We left soon after that to stay with Mom's mother for a few days while Mom healed physically and made plans to remove Jed from our lives. After we returned to our house, we had little left. Jed had broken in and destroyed almost everything. There was a lone undamaged chair surrounded by piles of other furniture and knick-knacks that he had meticulously destroyed. It broke my heart to see my mother cry again after all that she had been through, but even in the midst of such pain, I felt a glimmer of hope that my evil stepfather would finally be gone.

My real father was a tall, strong, good-looking, athletic man. He had been a boxer while in the Army and had acquired quite the reputation as a street fighter in our town after he returned. He had an equal reputation with the ladies and made no attempts to hide it from my mom whenever he was drinking, often bragging of his conquests. I recall one night in particular, when Mom and I went out looking for him after he failed to return home. We found him drunk in a bar, up on the platform, dancing with a stripper. I must have been about three years old at the time.

It was also around that time that Dad decided to have some sick fun one evening when seeing me frightened by a monster on TV. He chased me into my bedroom where I'd fled to hide. Finding me under my small twin bed, he pulled me out legs first, kicking and screaming. He proceeded to carry me back into the living room to put me in a chair directly in front of the TV, holding my head forward and forcing me to watch what terrified me. He laughed at my fear, just as he had done a time before when holding me down on my bed with a pillow over my face until I was close to suffocating.

To him, it was funny. To me, it was traumatizing.

Soon after Mom and Jed split, Dad's dark cycle of torturous fun repeated itself when I went to stay with him and his longtime girlfriend Melissa for part of the summer in Saginaw, Michigan. Noticing that I would cover my face or leave the room every time the cable advertisement came on for the movie *The Exorcist*, Dad thought it would be humorous to once again force me to sit in a chair directly in front of the TV, while holding my head to watch. My fragile emotions from the years of severe abuse and trauma in my childhood war-zone were pushed over the edge and I could handle no more.

I began to wet my bed as I became absolutely terrified of the night. I would often hallucinate as the pictures on the walls and various items in my room evolved into frightening demons and monsters trying to kill me. Like a wartime soldier watching for his enemy, I hyper-vigilantly waited for sundown. It didn't matter where I was or what I was doing; when the sun began to set, my heart rate would soar, I couldn't concentrate, and I had the intense feeling of wanting to run and hide. I would lie awake almost every night until I saw daylight appear, and only then would I be able to fall asleep.

Upon returning to my home in Ohio, I found my already unpredictable world even more unstable, as my newly single mother had moved in her partying friend, Jed's sister Brandy, and Mom's younger brother Noah. Noah served as the live-in babysitter while Mom and Brandy went out drinking every night.

I soon became very difficult to handle, begging to sleep with my mom in her bed every night, but she was never there. One evening close to bedtime, Noah found me hiding crouched down in the bathtub, shaking violently like a frightened animal. With Jed gone, night time had become my new enemy. Brandy would often laugh at me and shame me when others weren't around, calling me a "little baby" and a "sissy boy." My hands eventually began to shake, making it difficult to complete the simple task of holding a glass of water with one hand.

Things became so bad that my mom eventually took me into see a child psychologist. After meeting with me alone, he suggested that my mom allow me to sleep on the floor at the foot of her bed at night. Hearing his words, I felt such a sense of relief. She followed through with that prescription, but when I saw her getting ready to go out again to the bars that night, all my hopes of safety went away. As I began to cry, reminding her of what the psychologist had said, she snapped at me saying, "Stop your crying! He said you could sleep on the floor by my bed but he didn't say I had to be in it!"

Even though I hadn't been able to count on my mom to protect me in the past, the internal instinct of wanting my mom in the midst of such growing fear and torment was still very much alive in me. I was a little boy who was immensely afraid and just wanted his mommy.

Fortunately, as I continued my activities with the little church, spent occasional weekends with my nurturing grandma, and started back to school, things began to get better. My emotions eventually stabilized to a more functional level.

The comforting smell of wood burning stoves, the colorful display of yellow, red, and green leaves on the trees, and the crisp, cool air made fall my favorite time of year.

Taking time to look around to ensure that no one was watching, I playfully ran and kicked a raked- up pile of leaves I saw in a random yard when walking home from school. I laughed as I cheerfully approached our house on Chester Street. "I hope there is more of that chocolate cake left that Grandma made," I thought as I turned the doorknob to enter our house.

"I'm baaack!" announced Jed with a Satanic smirk. I stood staring at him, coldly, with obvious shock and hatred. "You better wipe that look off your face, boy, before I wipe it off for you!" he blasted. "I told you: I own you, you little fucker. And there's not a damn thing you can do about it!"

CHAPTER 2

———— ✿ ————

ON THE FOURTH of July, while Mom, Jed, and their friends sat outside our duplex partying, my little friend Johnny and I decided to innocently explore each other's naked bodies under the sheets on the sofa bed in our living room. It was probably nothing more than boredom and curiosity from two four-year-olds who weren't ready to go to sleep, but when my mom came in and caught us, it turned into a deeply shaming experience that I never forgot. The shaming continued as my mom's best friend Lyla, of whom I was very fond, came over to visit the following day. Walking with me outside, she turned and said, "Shawn, your mom told me what you did last night with Johnny. That's gross and disgusting, and I won't be your friend anymore if you do something like that again, okay?!"

As heavy tears of humiliation began to sting my eyes, I dropped my head and nervously replied, "Okay, Lyla; I won't."

A year or so later, I was staying for the weekend with my grandmother in her second-floor, one- bedroom apartment. She had divorced Roy after catching him again with another woman. When I first arrived, she had a surprise for me: She had saved a large refrigerator box that had been used during her move. Together, we constructed a playhouse by cutting out a door and window with a box knife. My new pad was too big to be in Grandma's small apartment, so she let me keep it in the hallway directly outside her apartment door, at the top of the stairs.

I played in that box for so long that she allowed me to camp out in it overnight. Grandma always knew how to make things fun.

It was during this particular weekend stay that Grandma told me about Jesus. She said that Jesus was God's son and that He loved me so much that He had died for me and had risen from the dead. She explained that if I asked Him to forgive my sins and invited him to live in my heart, He would become my Savior, and I would go to heaven. Grandma's face lit up like a child on a carousel as she expressed how beautiful heaven would be, with no pain and suffering. I wanted so badly to go to this heaven Grandma described and leave the hell I was living in at home with Mom and Jed.

Later that evening, I went into Grandma's semi-lit bedroom by myself and knelt down on my knees by the bed. I folded my hands and asked Jesus to forgive my sins and to live in my heart. I was so excited afterward that I energetically ran out of the bedroom and yelled, "Grandma, I get to go to heaven!" She smiled and hugged me, expressing how proud she was.

The following evening while Grandma was distracted by a project in the kitchen, I sneaked into her bedroom to play dress-up. I wrapped her black crocheted shawl around myself tightly like a dress, and accessorized with her oversized red high heels, a strand of pearls, and a pair of clip-on earrings. Except for a wig and makeup, I was dressed in drag as nearly as a five-year-old boy could be. Unfortunately, I decided to strut out into the living room at the same time Grandma had opened the door for Jed, who had just arrived to pick me up.

Unaware of my fashion show, Grandma went directly back into the kitchen while Jed stood glaring at me with a look of death. Softly enough so that Grandma couldn't hear him, while over-enunciating each word with a devilish facial expression, Jed shook his finger at me and said, "Get your fuckin' ass in there and take that shit off! I better never catch you wearing shit like that again!"

My career in drag ended as soon as it had begun.

Afraid of being on her own, Grandma eventually remarried Roy and returned to the isolated country house. Although Roy remained faithful for a time, it didn't take long before he was once again up to his old bar-hoppin', womanizing ways.

The weekends I stayed with Grandma were among the happiest memories of those years for us both. We had an uncommon connection that was rare and beautiful.

"How'd you like your eggs, honey?" Grandma lovingly asked one Saturday morning as she began to heat up her black cast-iron skillet on the kitchen stove. "Sunnyside up, please, with no screen (my way of referring to the brown, crispy texture that forms on the outer edges of an egg when it is overcooked)," I quickly responded. "No screen, huh?!" Grandma laughed. "Okay, sweetheart, give Grandma a few minutes." With my ten-year-old, tired morning head propped up by one hand, I sat at the white oval kitchen table habitually chewing on several strands of my long blond hair, drawing imaginary animals with my finger pen on the red placemats. "There you go, sweetheart!" Grandma said, as she set a floral plastic plate with two perfectly cooked eggs and a piece of buttered wheat toast in front of me. "Thanks, Grandma!" I said as I eagerly began to eat.

As Grandma began to clean up the kitchen counter behind me, she calmly said, "Shawn? Did you know that there are places in the world where men marry other men and women marry other women?"

With wide, innocent eyes, I put my toast down and responded, "Really?"

"Yes, honey," she said, as she made her way to the chair beside me. With a serious yet sincere look on her face she continued as she sat down, "This is a horrible and wicked thing in the eyes of God, Shawn. The Bible says that these people, the homosexuals, will burn in hell and will forever be separated from God's love."

"That's horrible, Grandma!" I said.

"Yes, it is," she agreed. "You must never forget that homosexuality is a sin, and God hates sin!" she warned.

"You can't catch me!" yelled Scarlett, her long brown ponytail wagging behind her as she playfully dashed around the elementary school playground during recess. It didn't take long before I caught up to her and grabbed both of her arms from behind her back, bringing her to a halt. "Caught you!" I said victoriously. We both buckled over in laughter as we gulped the fresh spring air. "But you can't get me again," she snickered deviously before darting off a second time.

As a youngster, chasing the girls was something I really enjoyed. I loved the attention I received from them, and being really fast on my feet afforded me a boost of confidence each time I snagged one. I really liked girls and enjoyed spending time with them. They were fun, pretty, and sensitive—words that had often been used to describe me. I guess I related to girls in some way and felt more comfortable being myself around them. I had lots of girlfriends throughout my school years, but never kept one around for very long or allowed them to get too close.

Yes, I liked girls, but the hidden truth was, I also liked boys. I liked boys in a way that my Grandma and the preacher at the little white church said I shouldn't.

"Pull your pants down," said Keaton, as we played alone in my upstairs bedroom. "No, I don't want to get in trouble," I nervously replied, smiling. "Come on; no one will know," he said with a big, confident grin. I really wanted to, but the fear of being caught and shamed again was much stronger than my desire to give in.

"Pull 'em down!" he demanded with rising frustration. "No, I can't!" I said again, as my playful smile was quickly replaced by a look of inner turmoil. Seemingly unsatisfied with my answer, Keaton lunged aggressively towards me, trying to unbutton my pants. I quickly turned around and fell to the floor on my stomach as a maneuver to block his unwillingness to leave me alone. As he tried over and over to reach around me and unbutton my pants while I lay on the floor, I firmly held on to the waistband of my jeans just in case he succeeded. After several failed attempts to undress me, he eventually gave up.

Mad and frustrated, my schoolmate Keaton angrily shouted, "Stupid sissy, you're no fun; I'm leaving!" Little did he know, I was just as frustrated at the lost opportunity to fool around, but also relieved from my choking grip of fear and anxiety. Emotionally and physically exhausted from the struggle, I fell asleep on the floor, still lying on my hands.

The following Monday while I was walking home from school, Keaton and two older boys suddenly ran up behind me yelling, "Get the fag!" They chased me down the alley behind our neighborhood, and I ran as fast as I could through a neighbor's yard which extended to the front of their house on Chester Street. Before I could reach home, Keaton grabbed my hair and pulled me to the ground, punching and kicking me. I fought back as best I could until Keaton's two older brothers came running out of their house to separate us.

I was completely clueless as to why Keaton had turned on me in such a violent way. Time would reveal that it was the way he was dealing with his own homophobia and inner struggle with his sexuality. Sadly for us both, it was only the beginning of a tumultuous, perplexing, and enticing affair that lasted for several years. Although my continued interaction with Keaton might appear twisted to the outsider, abuse and violence were no strangers to me. They had become familiar aspects of my twisted childhood.

Keaton's dad Rufus was a mechanic and a drinking buddy of my step-dad Jed. Rufus, with his hillbilly accent and greasy appearance, would often smile at me and tell me how pretty I was with my long blond hair. Although he was always very nice and kind to me, I often felt awkward and uncomfortable in his presence.

Keaton's family lived several blocks from us on Chester Street in a filthy, rundown two-story house. In the hot, humid summer months, they would unconventionally cool their home by completely removing the front door. This also provided a standing invitation to every dog, cat, rodent, and insect in the neighborhood. The first time Keaton's older brother babysat my sister Hailey and me, I was terrified by the number of cockroaches crawling all over the walls and furniture. I felt the need to hyper-vigilantly scan the room the entire evening, trying to prevent one of these vile creatures from entering my safe zone.

Hailey and I had to spend a certain Saturday night at Keaton's family's house while Mom and Jed were out of town. Hailey slept on the sofa in the living room, while I slept with Keaton and his two older brothers in a queen-size bed in their back bedroom. After Keaton's brothers fell asleep beside us, Keaton rolled over on top of me. We eventually pulled our underwear down and fooled around most of the night. Even though this was highly pleasurable, I found it odd and annoying that Keaton kept whispering in my ear, "I wish you were a girl."

While Keaton and I enjoyed ourselves, one of his brothers woke up and looked directly at us. We instantly stopped all movement and pretended we were sleeping, even though it must have been obvious that I was lying directly on top of Keaton. Once the brother resumed snoring, we continued our playtime until we fell asleep. The next morning, Keaton's brothers teased us about our overnight extracurricular activities. Keaton angrily told them to shut up and stomped outside as Hailey and I gathered our things to walk home.

A week later, hot fiery flames incinerated the old shingled tool shed in our back yard that had been converted into my clubhouse. This act of arson was another painful strike of Keaton's inner rage.

I would often lie awake at night burning with sexual desire and fantasizing about Keaton. I was far too young and naïve at the time to understand all the complexities of our dysfunctional exchange: Keaton did what everyone else had done in my life: He hurt me.

The only places in my life that I had ever felt safe were with Grandma and inside the little white church, but as was the case for Keaton, a deep inner struggle with my sexuality brewed, creating within me a war that I had to win. It was a fierce battle to maintain and secure the conditional borders of love and safety that Grandma and the church provided. The condition of the treaty was clear: I could not be gay.

Instead of dealing with my inner struggle by inflicting pain and violence on others as Keaton did, I chose a path more socially acceptable but equally destructive, turning against myself. The gay part of me was officially declared as the enemy that must be divided and conquered. Toxic shame and self-hatred became my chosen weapons of self-destruction.

When I was in the sixth grade, my family moved across town. I heard through a friend some time later that Keaton had been locked up in a juvenile detention center. I never saw him again.

Waiting in front of Grant Middle School for the morning bell to ring, I could feel my adrenaline soar as I saw Larry and his crew suddenly walk around the corner of the large brick building. I quickly hid behind a much larger classmate, trying my best to avoid being seen. Standing there staring at the ground, I could see a dark, shadowy figure slowly approaching on my right. "Who you hiding from, dickhead?!" shouted Larry. As my school books went flying out of my hands, I could hear ripples of laughter coursing through the large crowd of students assembled on the school lawn. Larry kicked one of my books further out of reach as I scrambled to collect the others.

After retrieving my last book and clumsily standing to my feet, I felt a strange warm sensation flow through my body. I instantaneously felt stronger, bigger, and more alive! I somehow knew that if Larry approached me again, he would be sorry. Unfinished with his morning entertainment, Larry said, "Stay down, fag!" As he stepped forward to me push down, I confidently raised my right arm, firmly blocking his attempt.

The students loved it and began to laugh and jeer at Larry for not being strong enough. "I'm gonna kill you!" Larry screamed angrily as he came rushing toward me. Without notice, I took a right jab at Larry that sent him flying at least twenty feet into the bushes. The crowd roared and clapped as...

"Shawn? Shawn?!" said Miss Black.

"Huh?!" I stammered.

Greatly annoyed at my response, Miss Black firmly asked again, "What is the pronoun in the sentence I have written on the board?"

Having been abruptly ushered back from my fantasy of schoolyard heroism, I had absolutely no idea what she was talking about. As I sat there in complete silence staring at the blackboard, I felt light headed and nauseated, wishing I could disappear. After what seemed like an eternity, she rolled her eyes and strongly said, "*Pay attention* if you want to pass this class!"

Laughter began to ricochet around the classroom as the boy sitting directly behind me punched me in the back of my head, forcing me to slash through my tongue with the sharp edges of my teeth. I sat there stunned, tightly gripping my lips as the distinct rusty taste of blood filled my mouth. He chuckled, leaned forward, and whispered in my ear, "Stupid fag."

His words painfully reinforced what I had already begun to believe about myself: I was not smart, lovable, good looking, or normal. I was not enough.

I had struggled to focus in elementary school, but it was nothing like this. Possessing super-powers, singing before massive crowds, being popular with the girls: all were daydreams I created in my mind to escape from my present pain. The bullying, though? It was *real*. It was real and it hurt deeply; deeper than skin, deeper than blood. It didn't just hurt when I was punched, kicked, pushed to the ground, or chased all the way home. It hurt more when others laughed and stood by doing nothing, especially when it was those I thought were my friends.

"Run, Hailey! Run!" I shouted, trying my best not get frustrated with my little sister's attempt to make it to first base. Playing ball with our next-door neighbors was one of my favorite pastimes while living on George Street. Although the high number of previous broken windows and car dents had now restricted our baseball games to whiffle ball, we still had a great time.

"Shawn! Hailey!"

Living in such close proximity to our neighbor's house made it easy to hear our mom's voice through the large bushes that divided our two backyards when she called. Since I was next up to bat, I decided to follow through with the oncoming pitch before responding to her. I swung the bat and made full contact, hitting the plastic ball over the garage and into the alley behind our houses. After confidently dashing around to all the bases to ensure our victory with my hands held high, I continued running directly into our back yard to meet our frustrated Mom, who was standing on the concrete step.

"Come on!" she said harshly, "I've been calling you! Come on in and use the bathroom and grab a drink; we're gonna go for a ride in the country."

Just the mere mention of "going for a ride," knowing that Jed would be driving, gave me heightened anxiety. I had a list of nightmarish memories of being trapped in the back seat of our car with Jed raging behind the wheel. His bipolar behavior would often change abruptly and off he would go, flooring the gas pedal, trying to escape his demons. One time in particular, following an argument with my Mom, he nearly flipped our car after a sharp right turn forced the car into a balancing act on the two right tires. I thought we were going to die. From that time forward, I struggled when getting into any car, no matter who was driving.

As we grabbed our things and headed out to the car, I noticed something really odd. Mom was carrying Shithead, our scruffy little black-and-white dog. Shithead was the name Jed had attached to him after we'd received the dog as a gift a few months before. Jed thought that he would house train this poor creature by beating him into submission. More times than not, this agonizing scenario usually played out the same way: He would beat the dog for urinating on the floor, forcing the dog to run away and hide. Jed would then call him, insanely expecting him to come running. The frightened little dog, shaking violently from fear, would slowly start to crawl towards Jed, as I would stand there begging the little dog over and over under my breath to please go to him. Too traumatized to respond, the dog would inevitably retreat back under the chair for safety, infuriating Jed. Jed would grab him, relentlessly beat him again, and throw him into the back utility room. Each time I would try to rush back there to console the little dog, Jed would say, "If you fuckin' go near that piece of shit, I'll do the same thing to you!" Jed wouldn't allow us to give the poor dog a proper name. He called him Shithead, saying that was all he was worth.

I identified with that fearful little dog, and it made me hate Jed more than ever.

"Why would Jed let Shithead come for a ride with us?" I wondered. "He must be in one of his happy moods."

It was a beautiful day as we drove out into the country—sunny, but not too hot. The summer had just begun and I could see large patches of wild dandelions growing plentifully on the side of the road. The sprawling branches of the towering oak trees seemed to wave at me in the back seat where Hailey and I sat.

When the car came to a stop in the middle of a desolate country road, my attention diverted to the front seat, where Mom was holding Shithead. Without saying a word, Jed grabbed the dog and threw him out the window. The car tires screeched loudly as Jed hit the gas to speed away.

Hailey began to cry as we both turned around, sitting up on our knees to look out the back window. We could see Shithead's little legs running as fast as they could, trying to catch up.

Shithead didn't yet realize that it was God's mercy that had thrown him out the window—but I did.

Lying on my bed one Wednesday after school, I angrily punched the wall over and over, screaming, "I hate this, God! I hate me! Why did you make this me this way! It's not fair, it's not fair!" Greatly frustrated, I grabbed my penis and continued my rant, "Why doesn't this work right? Why can't I be like all the other guys? Please God, I beg you, change me! Please change me!" Hot tears exploded from my eyes as I buried my face in my pillow.

My life was already difficult enough, and the added trials of puberty made it brutal.

I did everything I could think of to change my fate. I begged God continuously, I fantasized about girls, and I even tried masturbating while staring at a naked girl on a single torn-out page of a porn magazine. Nothing worked. I felt alone, frustrated, and more confused than ever.

To make matters worse, the only two places that I could retreat for an occasional short reprieve from my world of bullies were gone.

After she returned from the hospital for gall-bladder surgery, Grandma recognized Roy's weak attempt to hide the evidence of his having whored around in their home. This shattering realization, along with the constant rumors of his continued infidelities since they had remarried, proved more than Grandma could bear. Even so, she told my mom that she wouldn't leave Roy unless she caught him in the act.

The time of reckoning came late one Friday evening when a girlfriend of my mom's recognized Roy in a bar with another woman. Mom and her friend took Grandma to the bar, where she finally confronted Roy right in front of his mistress.

She left him and came to live with us, but she was never the same.

As for the little white church: Its deep legalistic beliefs requiring members to dress from a different era added to the immense pressure I experienced in middle school to fit in. This became far too great a burden for me, so I left.

When isolation and darkness seemed as though they would squeeze every last drop of life out of me, God's mercy came through once again. The seeds of creativity that had been planted within me years before, watered and nurtured by my grandmother, had begun to grow.

"I have a surprise for you today, class," Miss Kelly said with a smile. "I have discovered that your classmate Shawn has a beautiful singing voice, and I've asked him to sing for us today." As Miss Kelly sat down at the piano and began to play the intro to the song "The Rose," which she and I had rehearsed after school the previous afternoon, I quickly walked to the front of the class, closed my eyes, opened my mouth, and unwittingly changed the course of my life.

CHAPTER 3

THERE WAS AN explosion of excitement and jubilation in the megachurch auditorium in McAllen, Texas, as our drummer counted off and our seven-piece band began to play. As we picked up our microphones and moved into our set positions on the spacious stage, the energy and reaction of the crowd became a welcome deterrent against the intimidating bright lights and TV cameras. After a few minutes, my nerves subsided and I completely forgot that the cameras were there at all. As I finished leading the first several up-tempo praise songs, I prompted Rita, our dynamic Latina alto to step forward and begin the next number. The audience erupted in cheers, recognizing Rita as one of their own. She had grown up there and had been an active member in that church for several years before auditioning for our group in Dallas.

We then featured our multi-talented violinist and the band in an Irish instrumental dance song, a crowd favorite wherever we performed it. Andrea and I both took opportunities to exhort the congregation, as we begin to transition into a much slower-paced set of worship ballads and powerful solos from a few of our gifted singers. So often, I would feel chills when our angelic soprano from England would sing; tonight was no different. Many people voluntarily knelt down in humble response to this tender moment.

Contemporary praise and worship was the group's greatest strength and had become our hallmark style. Incorporating songs from the prominent worship bands of Australia and the United Kingdom helped give the group a more updated, edgier sound and an ability to connect with a much younger demographic. No doubt, there had been nights in our three-month summer tour when the crowds were much smaller and the people were not responsive at all, but this night was not one of them. This night was extraordinary: a sacred space where all-out physical expression met complete reverence; where high praise turned to intimate reflection and meditation in silence. It was a holy night I will never forget. During rare moments like these, I felt I was exactly where I was supposed to be, doing exactly what I was supposed to be doing.

The training institute and organization that we represented provided a colorful mélange of international peoples and cultures. With as many as seventy different nations represented on campus at one time, it created a unique opportunity for our group to have a notable multicultural sound and presence.

When I stepped into the position as director of the band, it was shockingly apparent that we had to both raise this sinking ship from its dreary morass and completely turn it around into uncharted waters. I knew that this would require a strategically calculated, radical approach.

I challenged everything the group had been doing over the past decade and methodically did away with most of it. The aging internationally recognized co-founder of the organization, who had been publicly referred to by a prominent Christian leader as "the woman Moses of our time" was out of touch and one of our biggest obstacles to the vastly needed changes. To her, the group had become a sacred cow that she didn't want put out to pasture. I had to call upon the director of the institute more than once to skillfully intervene on our behalf. It paid off and once again, the group began to attract some amazing talent. In only eighteen months, we created one of the most polished albums the group had produced in its twenty-five year existence. It wasn't a commercial success by any means, but it was a considerable step forward in repairing the group's badly damaged reputation.

Early the morning after the holy night at the megachurch, as the Pastor retrieved Andrea and me from the hotel, we loaded the group and our luggage into our forty-two-foot blue tour bus. Our faithful driver Robert and his sweet wife Ellen had arrived early and had things ready to go, as was their custom. Overseeing the bus was a taxing responsibility at times, but I could always depend on Robert to help. He had become a dear friend to me and I had grown to respect him greatly. He made the eleven thousand miles of travel in the summer so much easier. With the typical week consisting of five concerts, often in various states, I couldn't have managed without him. I would often sit in the semi-isolated front passenger seat to read and study, or sometimes work on a new lyric for a song I was composing. This mobile office with a view provided me the needed space away from the rest of the team to stay productive and to meditatively recharge.

Traveling could be exhausting at times, but there was something remarkable about being on the road. Meeting unique people, experiencing unfamiliar places, learning unusual things—a new adventure unfolded every day. Between the concert dates and events, we also scheduled time off for fun and exploration. Andrea and I reverted to big kids when it came to sightseeing and visiting historical places, while beaches, shopping, and amusement parks were often a big hit with everyone else.

To keep everything running smoothly and effectively in our home on wheels, Andrea created a rotational operations schedule in which everyone took part. One day, Elsa, our shy and timid international flute player from Poland, was scheduled to clean the restroom before we arrived at our next destination.

Deep in meditation and prayer, I found myself suddenly jolted by a blood-curdling scream coming from the back of the bus. As I jumped up out of the front passenger chair and hurdled toward the back of the bus, I heard the restroom door swing open with a bang.

"Somebody poop-ded!" screamed Elsa with her heavy Polish accent. "Somebody poop-ded on the seat of toilet!"

I could see Tom and Scott laughing hysterically out of the corner of my eye. We had a rule that the restroom on the bus could be used only for *number one*, never number two. Fully aware that sweet, innocent Elsa was next in line to clean the restroom, Tom and Scott (our team pranksters), had chewed up a portion of a chocolate candy bar and placed it on the toilet seat for Elsa to find. I had to admit it was pretty clever and we all got a good laugh out it, including gullible Elsa.

As our tour bus pulled up to the ten thousand-seat coliseum in Shreveport, Louisiana, for our final booking of the summer tour, excitement ran high. We were about to lead worship for one of the most successful and controversial evangelists of the day. This South African evangelist was dubious because of the strange breakouts of uncontrollable laughter that would erupt throughout the immense crowds at his international crusades. Even so, throngs of people poured in because of the high number of reported healings that were taking place. We tried our best to not judge and to remain indifferent when performing at events of this nature. We were there because we had been invited, and of course for the exposure it would bring to the institute. Our group knocked it out of the park once again. The tangible energy in the expansive venue was an undeniably connecting force that drove us into God's presence. It was another heavenly night.

There was such a favorable response from the crowd that the evangelist and his wife wanted to meet with Andrea and me after the event to discuss the possibility of working together again. He informed us that the night before, he'd had one of the most recognized Christian singer-musicians in the world lead worship and there had not been half the response from the people as with our group. We left the meeting humbled and astonished at how far we had come.

Being the youngest member of the faculty at this internationally recognized institute should have given me a sense of accomplishment and honor, but I was too tense and full of anxiety to enjoy this particular moment. I felt so small and insignificant as I glanced around the large conference room full of distinguished faculty and governing leadership. Like an imposter, I was afraid that someone would recognize my displacement and hurriedly usher me away. Even after all the ministry experience I had accumulated, the uncomfortable struggle when being in the presence of senior authority remained. I could feel my knees and hands quiver but tried my best to hide it. As time went by, my confidence did grow, but deep down inside, I never did feel like I was enough.

Teaching classes and leading worship at the Institute was an honor beyond words for me. It was a humbling and unique platform from which to influence and educate students from around the world, knowing that one day they would return to their nations of origin and teach what they had been taught. It was an exceptional moment to mentor the leaders of leaders, with the realization that in some small way, I had the honor of adding to their value and development. Coming from my lowly background and position in life made it even more special. My students provided the affirmation and encouragement that I lacked in my marriage. I drew such strength and energy from their loving hearts and seemingly endless capacities to learn and grow. They were my daily doses of inspiration.

To lead worship at the institute was a worship leader's dream. Some of the best-known worship songs in the world had been born there. Every morning we would gather for chapel, and that's where the magic would happen. The students were continuously responsive and often came with a high level of anticipation. Maybe it was because of what it had taken for many of them to get there, and the tremendous amount of sacrifice it required of them. I remember one international student telling me that when he decided to attend the institute, he was disowned by his wealthy Muslim father. Later, he was contacted by a close friend who warned him that his father had a death contract out on him; he would be killed if he returned to Bangladesh. Even in the midst of such hatred and turmoil, this young man was full of love and forgiveness. This was only one of many courageous stories I heard during my time teaching at the institute.

Our travels and ministry experiences with this organization carried Andrea and me to almost every state in the country, as well as to Canada, England, Scotland, Ireland, and Belgium. Speaking and leading worship on our tours gave us both the coveted opportunity to refine our skills as public speakers and performers in multifaceted venues. We had rare opportunities to minister in some of the largest churches in the country, as well as in some that were just getting started; building meaningful relationships with internationally known leaders, songwriters, and authors; and taking time to encourage and lift up those who were struggling, believing their dreams had passed them by.

My decision to work for this organization had required a decrease in salary, but what I received back from the invaluable experiences and relationships was worth far more than money.

"I really appreciate your taking the time to have lunch with me today, Mr. Nemeth. I value the input and insight you have given me."

Mark had always been very respectful toward me and he looked up to me as a mentor and trusted friend. He was one of the singers in the group and had been traveling with us for a few years at that point. Admired and appreciated by his peers in the group, Mark could always be counted on when someone was in need. He was a natural leader and had developed a sizable following of his own at his local church as an associate pastor for single adults.

As we climbed back into my car after finishing our lunch, Mark turned to me and said, "Mr. Nemeth, before we leave, can I talk to you about one more thing?"

"Sure," I said. "What's on your mind?" I could see on his face that he was a little nervous and I smiled to reassure him.

"I hope I have proven myself to be one that you can trust, and I have always tried my best to be respectful to you and Mrs. Nemeth both."

"Absolutely, Mark, you can talk to me about anything," I said.

"There is no easy way to say it, so here goes. During our tour, when Mrs. Nemeth and you stayed at my parents' home, my mother commented to me about her disgust with Mrs. Nemeth's behavior toward you. Some of us in the group are really struggling with this also. I know that she is your wife and that's why I have hesitated for some time now to say anything at all. She is demeaning to you, and talks you down even when you are not present. When you have her lead rehearsals, she often undermines the direction you have already given. Several of the girls have had ongoing personal issues with her, too. She is obviously jealous of them and a few of them are considering leaving the group as a result. Please forgive me if I have crossed the line, but we love and respect you and I couldn't hold back from saying anything any longer."

The loving concern and compassion expressed so earnestly in Mark's words beat against my walled-up emotions like an iron pillar. I broke. I melted into the steering wheel and sobbed uncontrollably. In front of my student, I shouldn't have; yet, to relieve the pressure of three long years of unspoken emotion, I couldn't hold back.

Mark's words were only the tipping point that triggered an avalanche of deep, hidden pain and frustration against which I seemed to have no control. Much more went on behind the scenes than I'd disclosed to anyone. I felt intensely isolated and alone. Not even my closest friend, who had been my best man in our wedding, knew the full details. I believed that my role as Andrea's husband was to protect her and that I would be dishonoring her and failing to trust God if I talked to anyone else. But inwardly, the growing resentment and anger chipped away at the anchor of hope to which I was clinging and the desperate belief that things could change.

As a teacher and speaker, Andrea was fantastic—one of the most gifted at the institute. I often had people approach me on campus expressing to me their gratitude for the insightful and enlightening class they had attended with my wife as teacher. She amazed me with her ability to speak extemporaneously when called upon. She was a natural at this, and far better than I was. I tried my best to encourage her where she was most gifted and to praise her in her strengths, believing that she would be most successful in those areas. Despite the fact that she had not studied music on a university level, Andrea was a talented worship leader, and her skills had served her well in the circles of ministry that focused more on passion than on musicality and polished detail. By professional standards, though, her musical abilities were limited; worse, she was unwilling to acknowledge this and accept any constructive criticism. I grieved so much over the continual struggle it created between us.

The producer of our first album wanted to cut Andrea's song because of all the pitch issues. I knew he was right but I told him that he had to make it work.

"I can't do that to her," I said. "She's my wife." I suggested that he bring a couple of the other singers back into the recording studio to even out the problem spots with layered vocals. He also wanted to cut Andrea's vocal part from another song that I had written and recorded, but instead, I had him pull her down in the vocal mix to lessen the areas of concern. When Andrea heard the final mixes, she criticized me harshly on the changes made, accusing me of trying to sabotage her.

Several months later, the director of the recording label at the organization wanted me to work with Andrea on her piano playing. He said it was too "old school" and needed to be simplified. Instead of talking to her himself, he wanted me to deal with her. Even though

I tried my best to walk softly and encourage her on the adjustments, she resisted.

Andrea was completely unaware that anyone else had spoken with me about her musicianship. I thought it would be cruel and heartless to tell her. Instead, I was secretly trying to guide and encourage her into the needed changes while allowing her to maintain some dignity. It backfired and only added to her belief that I was against her. How ironic that I was actually trying my best to support and stand up for her. I couldn't win.

Time after time, I would hear about Andrea's anguish over my decision to assign a solo to another woman instead of her. I reminded her again and again that our purpose was to mentor and develop these students for professional careers in music ministry, not to make it all about us. It never seemed to register. Throughout our marriage, she would leave long, carefully constructed letters on my desk expressing her disapproval of my leadership, and lists of areas she wished I would improve upon at home. She would often hold me to the standards of more-seasoned ministers who were fifteen or twenty years older than I.

The emotionally manipulative letters became exhausting, and seemed to pop up at times when I had been putting in extra-concentrated effort to make things better between us. I felt helpless to please her.

As I wiped my eyes with my shirt sleeve, I apologized to Mark for my outburst of emotion. He said, "There's no need to apologize, Mr. Nemeth; you are obviously in a lot of pain and in a very difficult position." Mark was so kind to run back into the restaurant to retrieve some paper napkins for me to clean my face before returning to the office.

What more could I say to him? My waterfall of despair had said everything. Things were not good, not good at all. I asked him to pray. "Please pray that things will change, Mark, and that God will give me strength."

He encouragingly replied, "I have been, and will continue to do so."

"If you marry this woman, you will ruin your life." The prophetic words from the therapist in California haunted me as I lay in bed night after night. And what about all the people I was so concerned about disappointing and letting down if I called off the wedding? None of them seemed to matter anymore. I had to live with the daily consequences of my actions. I was trapped in a marriage without intimacy, without passion. Yes, there were times that I longed to open up to Andrea and tell her of my lifelong battle with same-sex attraction, but sadly, I never felt like I could trust her. The way that she belittled me at times led me to believe that she would find a way to use it against me. I couldn't take the risk.

There is no doubt that Andrea and I were both full of hurt, anger, and disappointment. How could we not be? Neither of us had signed up for this.

CHAPTER 4

As I woke up that sunny Saturday morning in the quiet little house beside the church where I pastored, I felt a smothering wave of anxiety flood over me. I methodically put both feet down onto the floor, climbed out of bed, and made my way to the living room. With each step, I could feel the gnawing knot in my stomach draw tighter. I stood in front of the large brick fireplace unable to move; I was stunned, and somewhat in disbelief at what had taken place just a few hours before. The words came roaring out of me so loudly that it's difficult to recall if I actually said them or if it were just every cell within my body revolting: *"What did you do, Shawn?!"*

Overcome by emotion, I sat down in the nearby wooden chair and stared at the few remaining embers in the fireplace, the empty glasses on the mantle, the disarrayed pillows on the floor. They all bore witness of the baffling scenario. I had asked Andrea to marry me! I'd spent so many months wrestling in prayer about this decision and seeking the counsel of those I respected in leadership. I didn't take this lightly. Why, then, did I feel as if the very life had been pulled out of me?

Andrea and I had met in Dallas a few years before while we were both working for a large international Christian organization. She was six years older than I and was a seasoned minister in her own right. I had great respect for her as a teacher, speaker, and missionary. Andrea spoke four languages and could speak Spanish without an English accent. This was a noteworthy quality since she was a tall, white, blonde, blue-eyed girl from Colorado. She had lived in Mexico for several years developing a music school and had traveled extensively doing ministry work in several other nations. Over the course of time, we became friends and eventually co-led a mission team to South America.

As Andrea and I directed our group throughout Brazil, Argentina, and Chile, there was no denying that she and I made a very effective ministry team. We were both experienced, capable leaders and seemed to really enjoy working together. Our team had many notable opportunities to speak, lead worship, and perform dramas throughout all of these beautiful and captivating countries. The work that we had accomplished and the joy of carrying it out were electrifying; the response of gratitude from the people was unlike anything we had ever seen. But I must say that nothing touched me more deeply and impacted me more than serving and loving the forgotten children living in the trash dumps of Brazil. Coming from a country where we have such great abundance and take so much for granted, I was shockingly confronted with my own selfish and impoverished heart.

I will also never forget little Guillermo, the four-year-old boy with the big brown eyes whom I encountered in a rundown Catholic orphanage in Argentina. In a room full of overly excited children, I looked down to see his sad, dirty little face, his arms reaching up to me. How could I deny him?

I knelt down and scooped him up in my arms and there he stayed during our entire three-hour visit. He held on to me as if his life depended on it. Any attempt to put him down was in vain. He smelled of urine and poverty, but I didn't care. I saw myself in him. I sensed that just like me, he needed most to feel safe and wanted. As the rest of the children gathered around the team to watch the comical skits and to collect the colorful animal-shaped balloons, Guillermo remained completely content in his newly found safe place. When it was time to leave, the workers had to literally pry his little hands from around my neck and shoulders. Each scream I heard tore into my heart like a knife to paper. As we drove away I couldn't hold back the tears. I was so moved and troubled over leaving little Guillermo that I later discussed the possibility of adoption with the missionaries who had taken us to the orphanage. They explained that because I was not Catholic, I would never be considered a worthy potential parent. Guillermo has remained in my prayers ever since, always in my heart.

After the South American trip concluded, Andrea and I hung out for a few weeks back in Dallas before we both relocated to begin new leadership positions. She moved to Toronto and I moved back to Illinois, where I had pastored previously. We both found our new surroundings and the demanding, authoritarian senior pastors we worked with to be very disheartening at times. The loneliness and challenges of being single ministers encouraged us to take comfort in each other with late-night phone calls and reassuring letters. We identified with each other's circumstances, which made our friendship grow stronger and more meaningful. It was during this season that a blinding and twisted deception began to take root.

I knew that I had no physical attraction to Andrea. I had tried to entertain the thought, but I knew that it just wasn't there. One could argue that I didn't have it because I am gay, but I knew it was even more concrete than that. There had been a strikingly beautiful woman I loved before Andrea came along, and we had planned to marry. She was incredibly sweet, kind, and had a genuine, selfless heart for others. In so many ways, we were kindred spirits and I wanted desperately to open up to her about my inner struggle with same-sex attraction. I just couldn't. Shame was my prison. The tormenting frustration I experienced at loving someone so much and yet not desiring her sexually was crushing the life out of me. That had always been my dilemma and I hated myself for it. I had every intense and intoxicating emotion that one has when being in love, butterflies and all, but the sexual desire was nonexistent. I beat myself up for not being what I deemed "man enough." I knew if I married her, I could not be the husband she needed me to be, so I did the only honorable thing I believed I could: I broke her heart.

It was clear that I felt none of the captivating feelings for Andrea that I had experienced with my previous girlfriend, but with Andrea I was riding on an enticing cloud of future ministry potential. "If our amazing and fruitful trip to South America was any indication of what it could be like for us," I thought, "maybe it could work." Could ministry be enough? The crafty seed of deception was planted.

The thought of driving a moving truck with a car in tow for three thousand miles from Canada to California daunted me. But as we loaded the last remaining box from Andrea's apartment into the truck, I knew there was no turning back.

Having my heart broken wide open in South America for the hurting and indigent, I had sought to engage the church I worked for in Illinois with this same passion. I began to visit some of the poor single mothers in the community and acquired funding and mentoring for some of their children. However, my continued requests and endeavors did not always meet eye to eye with the senior pastor. After butting heads repeatedly, I realized that we did not share the same vision or values and it was time for me to move on. I decided to relocate to the San

Joaquin Valley of California to work for a church that had deep roots in missions work and caring for the distressed. The senior pastor and his family there had both served with Andrea years before on the mission field and had developed a very close relationship. Andrea and I both agreed that this move would be the best fit for us.

Prior to our tumultuous trek across the United States, I had moved to California and plunged into my new ministry responsibilities. California was a completely new culture for me as was the mindset of the people. I found the new challenge exhilarating. I greatly admired my new senior pastor. He was a fantastic orator, teacher, and counselor. Today, I attribute much of the skills and tools I utilize in speaking and wellness coaching to his mentorship. Over the course of closely working with me for several months, he wisely recognized that I had all the signs of clinical depression. He encouraged me to seek out a professional evaluation which could help determine if I had some sort of chemical imbalance. Even though I knew my engagement to Andrea was the source of my depression, I took my boss's advice.

The determined and firm look on the face of the psychotherapist gave every indication that she would not be deterred from pressing through my pastoral façade of smiles and positivity. She did. Her straightforward approach shook me to the core when she said, "If you marry this woman, you will ruin your life!" Dazed and perplexed, I responded to her, "You don't understand; I have no choice." From my self- imposed prison of fear, I sealed my fate.

In sad reality, I don't think that either Andrea or I felt we had a choice. In ministry work, if you're going to be taken seriously, marriage is inevitable. No one likes to admit it, but single ministers are considered second class in the hierarchy of evangelical ministry. We were often the center of people's shame-based conversations as to why we were still single. Prior to our engagement, feeling the pressure to marry was something we had discussed several times during our late night phone conversations. We were both tired of the game. Andrea had expressed that being an older woman was far more limiting to her leadership aspirations than I most likely encountered as a man. I knew she was right; ministry can be unfairly cruel that way.

A month before the wedding, after yet another long, drawn-out argument, I heatedly told Andrea that we needed to call off the wedding. Her newly exposed domineering behavior over the past several months had pushed me to my limit. As she ran out of my apartment, I felt as though my life was approaching utter ruin, but deep inside I also strangely felt relieved. Later that evening after we had both calmed down, she called, urging me to go through with my commitment. The guilt I sensed was too much and I gave in. All the red flags waved as bright signals telling us we shouldn't marry, but nothing seemed to stop us from the self-propelled momentum driving us to the matrimonial altar. The craziest thing of all: We had our first official date the night *after* we became engaged!

Anticipation, love, excitement, and *gratitude* are some of the common words I have heard expressed by people describing how they felt on their wedding day; for me, it was *fear.* My only hope was the deep-seated religious belief that as we said our vows, God would supernaturally transform me. For months I had been praying, meditating on Biblical passages, fasting, and believing that I would attain a passionate desire and sexual drive for my wife. I wanted it more than anything. I did not want to be gay!

Prior to the ceremony, Andrea wanted to meet with me in the sanctuary so that I could privately see her in her wedding gown before the pre-service photos. As I waited on the chancel, she entered from the back of the sanctuary while a pre-recorded love song that she had arranged began to play over the sound system. When I saw her, I couldn't move. Frozen, I thought, "This should be the happiest day of my life; it shouldn't feel this way." The scandal of feeling nothing for her was a torture beyond words. I felt numb, shameful, and surrounded by a profound sadness suffocating me like wildfire. To go through the motions was all I could do. Fortunately, I'd had to do that to survive so much of my childhood that I had already become quite skilled at it.

The beautifully decorated Dallas church filled up with our impressive list of international guests, esteemed ministers, and musicians. The mounting stress of it all was overwhelming me, and I tried my best to hide my need to run to the restroom several times to vomit. It must have showed, because the minister who was about to officiate the ceremony came back to check on me. I smiled, straightened my bow tie and said, "I'm fine." I had to be.

My brain was so frozen in dread that I remember very little of the ceremony. After the reception ended, Andrea and I collapsed in the back of the limousine. As we drove to the hotel, I knew the moment of truth was fast approaching. Did God change me during the ceremony? Would I be able to perform my husbandly duties? Apart from occasionally holding hands, sideways hugs, and a quick peck of a kiss now and then, Andrea and I had had virtually no physical contact of any kind before our honeymoon. Because of our very conservative religious beliefs, we were both virgins. I had never seen a woman completely naked before, except in magazines and movies. I was terrified. According to my friends, I knew that there was generally only one thing on the mind of most men after the wedding. The only thing on my mind was how to avoid it for another day. Nothing had changed. The honeymoon was a complete nightmare for both of us.

After several failed attempts to have sex with my bride, the pressure, anxiety, and shame became immeasurable. No woman deserves the intense rejection she must have experienced. I could hear her lying in bed crying and it ripped my heart out. With tears streaming down my own face, I lay in the dark and inwardly cried out to God for mercy.

Eventually, I was able to perform sexually throughout the rest of our marriage, but it never felt right or natural for me. It was emotionally painful and immensely traumatizing. If the tables were turned and society demanded that it was only acceptable for heterosexual men and women to marry and have sexual relations with their counterparts, I am completely convinced that their pain, disgust, and misery would not have been any greater than mine.

CHAPTER 5

GRINNING EVILLY AND looking at me through the corner of his eye, Jed's older brother DeWayne asked, "Jed, what are you going to do with this little fairy-boy?"

Chuckling under her breath, his plainspoken mother chimed in, "He should have been a girl; he's too pretty to be a boy. What you need to do is toughen the little fucker up."

I stood straight up with my back pressed against the dark-paneled dining room wall. I clasped my hands firmly behind my back while I gazed at the tattered area rug, trying my best to be invisible. Jed's family couldn't have cared less. His mom and siblings often talked about me as though I weren't even there. They were completely oblivious as to how their damaging words stabbed into my sensitive heart like a rusty knife poisoning my soul.

Jed's mother, who worked as a bartender, was a very perverted woman with the vocabulary of a trucker. It was from her that I first saw and learned what a dildo was, along with a few other sex toys. Her gruff behavior, raspy voice from years of chain smoking, and the large, protruding wart on the end of her nose combined into a witch-like persona. I was terrified of her. Jed's six brothers and sisters were obviously the products of their mother and would often abuse me with their vulgar words. Jed's younger brother Owen began molesting me from the time I first arrived in their home and continued for several years. One afternoon while he was babysitting me, he and a friend took turns on top of me sexually. I struggled with this for many years, tormented by the complicated mix of shame and sexual pleasure I experienced from such violation.

I hated going to their big, old house. Everything about its tawdry environment frightened and disgusted me. Jed's parents were hoarders, and the filth and odors in their home were absolutely nauseating. Piles of junk filled every space. The walls and furniture were covered with stains and thick layers of dust. Dirty dishes and cookware covered the kitchen counters, many containing the remnants of meals from days and even weeks before. Every one of my five senses was offended while I was there, and it usually took some time for me to relax enough to even sit down. Eating under such putrid conditions posed a real challenge. The long, wide upstairs hallway which led to the many rooms where I was often placed in bed with Owen for the night was furnished with trash, books, and magazines. In the pages of those discarded magazines, I discovered pornography.

Crying, I begged my mother to not take me to that house after the abuse began to happen. I related to her how cruel they were to me, and what Owen was doing to me at night. All I remember her saying was, "Shawn, what do you want from me?! I'll talk to them, but I have no other place to take you."

Nothing changed, and my unacknowledged suffering was replaced by a cruelly deafening silence.

"Why are you standing there? You're blocking the TV?! Can't you see I'm busy? Come back during a commercial!"

The angry, dismissive words of my mother pierced me like swords. I was such a sensitive little boy and by that time of my young life, so full of fear. Even though her harsh words hurt me, I wouldn't let them keep me from approaching her once again during the commercial break to ask the burning question that had been consuming my mind all day. I mustered up all the strength I could to approach her again and stood by her chair, waiting. When she turned to me with such a bothered look upon her face, I couldn't hold back my pent-up emotion any longer and my tears began to flow. Annoyed, she said, "Why are you crying?!"

Timidly but with conviction, I asked her, "Why don't you ever tell me you love me?"

I could instantly see her anger as she quickly blurted out, "What do you mean?"

I said, "I hear the parents of the other kids at school say how much they love them when they drop them off, but I never hear you tell me that. Don't you love me?"

In her anger and embarrassment, she told me she loved me, but her actions and demeanor washed away any hope I had of her answering my question and easing my pain. The truth was, she couldn't. She couldn't answer my question and for whatever reason, she couldn't love me. I have no memory of ever sitting on my mother's lap or of her demonstrating any kind of loving affection toward me. I remember only the deep torment of feeling unwanted.

As a child, I told myself that my mother's coldness towards me was because of my stepfather Jed. I would often hear them arguing about me. One night, they didn't realize that I was just in the next room and could hear everything they were saying. Jed expressed to my mom how much he couldn't stand me and wished I weren't there. Her response is forever etched into my soul. She said, "What do you expect me to do with him, Jed?" Perhaps most damaging was the way she said it, with a tone of being stuck with some unwanted baggage. I learned that night the tangible power we possess with our words as my mother handed over her parental rights in order to appease her husband. "Well then, you do with him what you want," she said. The words that she spoke that night became the prison of my existence for many years. Looking back, it makes a lot of sense why Jed seemed to have such a claim of ownership over me and why my mother seemed to have none. She had given me away. Jed would often remind me during times of abuse and violent outbursts that he *owned* me and there was nothing I could do about it. His actions portrayed me as a threatening enemy that he intended to conquer, or he treated me as though I existed only to answer his needs, as if I were a servant. He never seemed to recognize that I was only a terrified little boy who only wanted to be loved.

From that night forward, my mother seemed completely powerless to stop the abuse. If not powerless, she was definitely unwilling. I pleaded with her to protect me from the cruelty and torture I endured when she wasn't around. She didn't seem to care.

My first memory of Jed was when I was just four years old. My mother had separated from my father and we were living in an apartment. Jed was babysitting me while my mom was away and he decided to have some demented fun by getting me drunk.

I remember how funny he thought it was watching this little blond boy stumble around the apartment, crying for his mom and running to the bathroom to throw up. At sixteen, Jed was just a boy himself; my mother was in her early twenties. At the hands of my young mother and her teenage boyfriend, what chance could I have possibly had for any normalcy? The following weekend, I went to stay with my dad and told him what Jed had done. Dad left me with a friend and made his way to my mom's apartment, knocking the door flat off its hinges. He pulled Jed outside, where Dad proceeded to beat him to a bloody pulp. I carried the memory of that incident with me for many years, believing that Dad was my superhero and would protect me when I needed him.

In reality, my dad was an extremely violent man who on several occasions came close to killing my mother in front of me. As a result, by the time I was four, I was already severely traumatized.

The first occurrence happened shortly after my mom and dad had been fighting. While Dad was at work, Mom took me and we went to stay with her mother. It didn't take long for Dad to realize where we were and to furiously drive there to retrieve us. He took us out to a dark country road, locked me in the car, and pulled my screaming mother out by her hair. I was in the back seat banging on the window trying desperately to get out. As he dragged Mom off, I could see the knife. My heart was paralyzed by fear not knowing if I would ever see her again.

It wasn't until I was an adult that I learned that once they were out of my sight, Dad continued to drag Mom to a nearby bridge, where he hung her over the side by her ankles. He threatened to kill her if she ever left him again. Once Dad finished unleashing his anger, he took us home. Mom later expressed to me that what occurred that night initiated a turning point: She knew that Dad would eventually kill her if she *didn't* leave him, so she began taking the steps to separate from and ultimately divorce my father.

After much turmoil and police intervention, my mom and I eventually got away. We lived temporarily with my grandparents. I had been spending the weekend with Dad when Mom came to pick me up on a Sunday night. With virtually no warning, the innocent, carefree fun I was having while playing with my toy soldiers quickly evolved into a chaotic nightmare. My unpredictably volatile father pulled out a gun, pointing it at my mom's head. He said he wanted her back and forced her to beg for her life for what seemed like hours. I cried and frantically pleaded with him to stop. He picked up a decorative glass bottle from a nearby end table and threw it at Mom's head. As Mom blocked it from smashing into her skull, the bottle shattered everywhere, slicing her hand. It must have been the sight of the blood that eventually broke Dad free of his psychotic rage. He fell to his knees and started sobbing.

The superhero I thought would be there to protect me was chronically incapable. The continuous sting of waiting for him to pick me up on the weekends yielded only his empty promises to keep me company. The message grew eminently clear: I was *unwanted*. My superhero was nothing more than my fantasy to protect my mind from the real-life monsters. Even so, I did everything I possibly could to keep the fantasy alive by reminding my wicked stepfather Jed of my dad's impending doom if Jed touched me. It worked for a while, until Dad relocated to another state. After that, I remained completely at the mercy of one who seemed to be my greatest foe.

In a single night, the twisted culmination of all my childhood fears was magnified tenfold when I heard the blood-curdling screams of my mother and sister end with gun fire. I instantly jumped out of my bed, knowing that I had only seconds before Jed got to me. The pounding of my heart was nearly as loud as the screams of my mother and sister. *"Should I hide?"* I wondered. No; Jed would find me for sure. I quickly took the only option I had: I flung the bedroom door open and ran! As I reached the top of the carpeted staircase and began to descend, I heard Jed's heavy steps on the creaking floor behind me. I missed a couple of the stairs but caught myself on the wooden banister before I tumbled any farther. I realized my hurried escape from this madman was all in vain when once again I heard the gut-wrenching sound of gun fire. My lifeless body tumbled to the bottom of the stairs.

Suddenly, my eyes flew open and I sat straight up in the bed. "You're okay, Shawn," I said out loud, calming myself as I'd had to do night after night from this hellish recurring nightmare. As I looked around the room, I immediately felt a comforting peace flood over me. "I'm at Grandma's house!"

I was safe. With that tranquilizing realization, I gently fell back to sleep, smiling.

The next morning, I woke up to the comforting sound of playful birds chirping outside my window, and the tantalizing smell of bacon and eggs frying in Grandma's kitchen. Food was often scarce at home because of my parents' party lifestyle, but I never had to worry about hunger—or anything else, really— when I stayed with Grandma. Her skill in the art of country cuisine brought her great delight in preparing all my favorite foods. Grandma and her husband Roy raised a good portion of their food and everything was so fresh and flavorful. Roy, an avid hunter and fisherman, kept the freezer stocked with wild game and fish, along with the beef and chicken they raised. Being such a curious child, I was often up for the challenge of trying something new, like possum stew and pickled cow brains.

After breakfast that morning, I hopped up into Grandma's lap in her pillowed wooden rocking chair by the window, as I often did. As we sat face to face, I playfully squeezed her arms as I eagerly listened to her recite her favorite nursery rhymes with great animation and dramatic effect. Grandma was a gifted storyteller and I never tired of hearing her. She was equally talented as a singer and often serenaded me in her sweet country voice. She loved George Jones, Elvis, Dolly Parton, and Christmas music. Passion and appreciation for music, storytelling, and classic black-and-white movies were some of the greatest treasures that Grandma instilled in me. One year for Christmas, I received a tape recorder and captured hours of her unmatchable singing and storytelling. I labeled the cassette "Grandma's Greatest Hits." What a source of comfort and assurance I found in endlessly listening to that cassette when we were apart. Grandma's voice was a light in my darkness.

Grandma and Roy lived in one of only four houses on a quiet country road in rural Ohio, about fourteen miles outside of our town. My mom's biological father had died from cirrhosis of the liver because of alcoholism when she was eleven years old. I recall Roy being grumpy most of the time and not very friendly. What I remembered enjoying most about him was his absence. One thing I knew for sure, even at such a young age: He didn't deserve my grandmother. Grandma made everything and everyone around her look and feel better. She had a kindness and sweetness about her that was completely disarming, genuinely honest, and undeniably infectious. With her dark brown hair and warm smile, she was pretty, well dressed, and always smelled wonderful. She looked much younger than her physical years, a genetic trait on her side of the family.

As an underprivileged child, I thought my grandparents were wealthy. They lived in a red-brick, white-trimmed ranch-style house that they had built on about two acres of semi-wooded land. The land was meticulously manicured with flower gardens of tulips, daffodils, and geraniums, including an extensive vegetable garden and fish pond where my little sister Hailey and I frequently swam when we visited. Roy had built a white wooden fence that outlined the front of the property bordering the blacktop country road. A skilled carpenter, he also constructed a striking ranch-style wooden arch over the long driveway, with their name featured in glossy black wooden letters; along with black-and- white benches, picnic tables, and flower boxes creatively scattered throughout the property. Compared to my own very modest surroundings, visiting my grandparents was equivalent to staying with the Ewings at South Fork!

Visiting Grandma's house cultivated within me a deep love and gratitude for the outdoors and nature. I would often wander off for hours and become temporarily lost in the nearby dense woods or cornfields on one of my afternoon adventures. On one particular excursion, I discovered a shallow, rapidly flowing creek between two corn fields. The somewhat narrow creek was full of colorful rocks, small fish, and frogs. When the rain was sparse and the creek was minimally full, I could jump from one side to the other, but after a bountiful downpour, I would have landed squarely in the middle. My unlimited curiosity drove me to accumulate the personal experience to back up this measurable assessment many times! The local farmers had built a narrow wooden bridge across the creek that allowed their tractors to cross during planting and harvest seasons.

One Saturday after school had just let out for the summer, I rode my yellow bike down to the grassy overgrown path that led to the creek. I was sitting on one side of the bridge throwing rocks into the water below when I noticed three unfamiliar faces coming my way. It didn't take long before these friendly siblings struck up a conversation and eagerly invited me into their enchanted world of childhood fun and innocence. Logan was the oldest at 16, Tabitha was 14, and Violet was 11. They said they lived in the old white farm house down the road with their parents and four other brothers and sisters.

Logan was strong, fearless, and witty. It was fairly easy to gauge that he loved to push all boundaries and would seemingly try anything, often before even thinking about the consequences of his actions. Violet, with her bouncy brown locks, freckle-painted face, and deep Southern drawl, was carefree and full of life. Sweet, pretty, and mature was the best way to describe Tabitha, who was obviously the most responsible of the three.

While we all were sitting under the bridge to escape the summer sun, Logan noticed a bird's nest attached to the side of the bridge towering over us. Without thinking, he threw a rock to see if he could hit it. He hit it, all right! The small, fragile nest, baby birds and all, crashed down to the creek below. The girls and I yelled at Logan for his recklessness as we frantically rushed to retrieve the newborn cargo. It was of no avail; before we could rescue the nest full of nature's gifts, they were quickly washed downstream and out of sight. It took some time for me to get over the misfortune of these tiny helpless creatures. How could Logan be so cruel?! I was somewhat relieved to hear that Logan got a good whipping for his carelessness when Tabitha and Violet told their dad what their brother had done.

Before we concluded our introduction, Violet, with her legs tightly crossed, said she had to relieve herself and couldn't wait. I laughed as she quickly hobbled back behind a nearby bush to unashamedly do her business. When she returned to the rest of us, Tabitha leaned over and quietly asked her how she'd cleaned up without the use of toilet tissue. Violet nonchalantly responded, "I just pulled the leaves off the plant beside me and they worked mighty good." Little did she know at the time that the plant she had used for her personal hygiene was poison ivy. I was informed later that the poor thing suffered for days because of her innocent blunder.

The trio and I met down at the creek several more times before I went home with them to meet the rest of their family. This unrefined country clan, originally from Kentucky, became my favorite playmates during my pre-adolescent years. They were exciting, funny, and always up for a new adventure. We would often play tirelessly for hours, picking wild berries by the creek, racing our bikes on the vacant country road, or chasing each other in a game of tag or hide-and-seek. They fascinated me with their unbridled agrarian lifestyle, with chickens in the house, a pet raccoon, and a country twang strong enough to rival the Clampetts on *The Beverly Hillbillies*. Yet, they were a very talented musical family and had assembled their own gospel singing group. They would often perform in various camp meetings, churches, and festivals. I can recall many afternoons when we sat around the antique upright piano in their living room and freely sang at the top of our lungs. This kind and loving family helped instill within me a passion for singing and performing. I listened to their gospel album over and over when I was alone and encouraged myself with the inspiring words and melodies that flowed from their music. They were completely unaware of their impact on my life and the greatly needed escape they provided me from my world of pain and sadness. I am so thankful for their imprint on my heart.

The anticipation and excitement I felt before a weekend at Grandma's was on par with the night before a coveted trip to an amusement park. Maybe it was just the simple fact that while spending time with her I got to experience, even for a short time, what it felt like just to be a kid, to have that extraordinary opportunity of basking in the sustaining freedom that only uninhibited spontaneity can create.

It seemed as though Grandma had meticulously prepared for hours before each visit on how she could fashion our limited time together to be the most enjoyable and exciting experience ever. I'm sure it was just Grandma being Grandma, but to me it was magical.

Grandma must have recognized my artistic abilities and love for creating things. I'm not sure when the tradition began, but I clearly remember running to the hallway closet to peek into the large box of goodies that Grandma had been collecting for me. Each time I eagerly looked into my cardboard treasure box, I was never disappointed to find newly added items like brass buttons, small cigar boxes, and colored construction paper waiting for me.

Creating things with my hands was very therapeutic for me and I would often spend hours sprawled out on the green-carpeted floor of the guest bedroom cutting, drawing, and formulating some sort of childhood masterpiece. This creative flow had become an effective way that I comforted myself and steadied my traumatized emotions. I carried this healthy behavioral practice back into the darkness of my childhood home by spending hours locked up in my bedroom rearranging the furniture and reenacting the colorful vivid scenes I saw played out in the movies.

I recall building a single-story house made of paper, Elmer's glue, and cardboard boxes. I scrupulously designed and decorated each room, one by one. Grandma would sometimes come in to sit with me and enthusiastically ask me questions about what I was building. She would also often have to lovingly prompt me to break long enough from my architectural composition to enjoy a sandwich and chips before continuing with my creative burst of obsession. Otherwise, I would have stayed in there all day.

In the evening, Roy would often head into town to the American Legion or his favorite bar while Grandma and I indulged in a classic-movie night with some of her famous homemade chocolate popcorn. We loved old movies, especially the ones with Cary Grant and Jimmy Stewart. Grandma would sometimes reminisce during the commercial breaks about going to the picture show for a dime when she was a little girl and how much simpler life was then. Nobody could tell a good story like Grandma! Other times, she and I sat outside under the stars, making s'mores, singing, and talking for hours around a blazing fire in the large stone fire pit that Roy had constructed.

Grandma was unselfishly affectionate towards me and I drank in her love like the parched summer grass consumes a nourishing rain. To me, my grandmother was sunshine. She was the most beautiful song that never gets old, played over and over again. She was a nurturer, a healer, a childhood companion, an inspiring creative teacher. She was a gift to me.

As little Josef came running around the corner of the old two-story barn chasing a field mouse, he caught a glimpse of his older brother Tomas and sister Aranka arguing beside one of the large stacks of hay. Experience had taught him to stay out of sight when his siblings were going at it, so he quickly hid. Aranka was yelling at Tomas in Hungarian and Tomas was trying to calm her down in English. Everyone in their large Catholic family could speak both languages except Mama; even so, Josef couldn't figure out what they were so mad about. It didn't take much to get Aranka upset, and when she was, everyone around her proceeded with caution. For some time now, Josef had heard strange stories from several of his eight brothers and sisters about Aranka that didn't seem to make sense, but none of them had prepared him for what he was about to witness.

Tomas must've given up trying to dissuade Aranka with his words, as he frustratingly pushed her into one of the towering stacks of hay nearby. After quickly reaching down to grab his pitchfork, he angrily stomped away. Tightly clinching her fists and lips, Aranka sprang to her feet in defiance. She walked purposely to the center of the field, surrounded by the large haystacks Tomas had been laboriously arranging for the past two days. Standing tall with her feet wide apart, she bent all the way over, clutching both of her ankles. As she looked through her legs upside down with her long, dark, wavy hair almost touching the ground, she yelled into the wind with an ominous tone, "Witchy, witchy, blooow!"

A few seconds later, Josef almost jumped out of his skin when hearing his sister Aranka wildly scream out the same perplexing phrase with greater force: "WITCHY, WITCHY, BLOOOW!"

Suddenly, a violent wind came ripping through the field. Josef ducked for cover, frantically pulling over his head a section of unused canvas that covered an old pile of firewood.

When the wind calmed and Josef climbed out of his makeshift storm cellar, there wasn't one stack of hay standing in the spacious field. It looked as though Tomas had done nothing at all to complete his two-day work assignment. And unfortunately for Tomas, that was exactly what Papa thought, too. Papa didn't care that Tomas was almost a man; he gave that boy the whipping of his life!

At the dinner table that evening, while Papa continued to scold Tomas, Josef sheepishly looked down to the other side of the table at Aranka. She saw him and smiled deviously, as if to let Josef know she knew he'd been there in the field that day all along, watching.

Over the years the mysteries about Aranka multiplied, and the legend of her witchcraft grew with each new story. Aranka always did things her way, so when Papa lost his farm during the Great Depression, she used her greatest natural asset—her beauty—to support herself. To her, it wasn't selling herself; it was refusing to let the circumstances of life defeat her. Aranka refused to let anything or anyone control her, and giving away the twenty children she bore through the years was her way of letting everybody know it. Although she married numerous times, several of her abusive husbands were eventually found dead: stabbed, shot, hit by a train.

Dad often told me stories like these about his Aunt Aranka when I went to Michigan to visit him. The times I was around her, I mostly kept my distance. The hard life she'd lived was clearly evident within the many deep lines on her face, circling her unusually crooked nose that had obviously been broken a time or two. Her deep, raspy smoker's voice made her all the more frightening to me.

My grandfather Josef had told Dad that his parents' family in Hungary had been gypsies. Being schooled in the dark forces of magic and sorcery from watching too many vampire and warlock movies as a child, I naturally wondered if that had something to do with Aranka's witchcraft. "Could she have somehow found a way to tap into some dark generational pool?" I wondered. Having personally experienced what he believed to be Aranka's wrath, Dad seemed to think so. When he was much younger, he had an argument with Aranka one night over the phone while hanging out with some friends at a local bar. As he walked home shortly after midnight, he was attacked and stabbed by a group of guys who left him for dead in a dark alley. He eventually made it to the hospital before bleeding to death. Had Aranka put a hex on him?

The last unusual story I recall hearing about Aranka took place at the rural home of one of her sons whom she'd given to Mama and Papa to raise. I remember being there a few times with my cousins, playing hide-and-seek around the trees and riding on their three-wheelers through the ditches. According to Dad, it was a weekend night like many others, with lots of drinking, laughing, and arguing. But this time the argument between Aranka and her son got out of hand. She supposedly got so mad that she walked away from him and locked herself in his bedroom, refusing to come out for hours. When she finally reappeared, without saying a word to anyone, she got into her car and drove home. In the middle of the night while everyone was asleep, the house caught fire and burned to the ground. All of my cousins made it out alive, but some of their pets were not so fortunate. The family lost everything.

I found Dad's Hungarian side of the family peculiarly fascinating, and yet strangely familiar. They would often sit around drinking, laughing, and speaking in Hungarian, which I didn't understand. But something in me felt right at home with their unreserved, dramatic, passionate ways of expressing themselves. When I was at home with my mother, she often scolded me for talking too much, but when I was with Dad's family, I fit right in.

The men in my father's family loved to fish and hunt, and many of the memories I have with them revolve around a fishing pole and a wiggling worm. Overnight fishing trips were among my favorite activities with them. The thrill of it had nothing to do with the fishing, which I thought was boring, and more to do with just being out in nature. While they were fishing, I would often keep the fire going by searching for dead branches nearby. Dad's younger brother Sam, probably the most obsessed fisherman in the bunch, still always somehow found time to sneak away and hide in the bushes to scare me.

Probably what I observed and appreciated most about my Dad and Grandpa was their strong work ethic. They were both blue-collar workers who put in a lot of hard hours for everything they had. Grandpa retired from thirty-five years of back-breaking service at a steel mill in Marion, Ohio. I respected the fact that although he had acquired only a third-grade education and never learned to read and write, he still did all he could to support his wife and five children. Even after retirement, it was rare to see him sitting idle. He always had a project of some sort in the works.

On one of my trips to Michigan to spend the summer with Dad and his longtime girlfriend Kelley, Dad was suddenly laid off from his job. Until he could secure new employment, he decided to lean on an old craft his father had drilled into him as a boy: boxing. Even though it was extremely dangerous, Dad began to fight for an underground boxing organization in Detroit with a bunch of thugs. His parents moved to Michigan so Grandpa could manage him. The money was good but the damage to his body was brutal. Eventually, he landed a well-paying job with General Motors, and was fortunate enough to leave boxing behind before the damage became too severe.

When I was twelve years old, things had gotten so bad between my stepfather and me that I moved to Michigan to stay with Dad and Kelley for about six months. It was the beginning of my summer break, just before seventh grade, and I was looking forward to starting a new chapter in my life, free from the tumultuous environment with Jed. Driving to the store to pick up some ice cream one Saturday afternoon, Dad turned to me and nonchalantly said, "Shawn, you're starting to become a man, I think it's about time that I take you to visit a prostitute."

"What?!" I said, in complete shock. "I don't want to do that!"

He started laughing and replied, "Shaaawn, it's okay, it'll be good for you. Grandpa did the same thing with me when I was about your age."

I quickly reverted to the fastest way I could think of to keep Dad from following through with what sounded like a disgusting idea: I quoted scripture. My diversion worked! Greatly annoyed whenever I talked about my Christian beliefs, Dad dropped the subject and turned up the radio. I'd dodged a bullet.

A few weeks later, on Sunday evening about an hour after dinner, Grandpa Josef asked me if I wanted to go with him to a local bar he often frequented to play a few games of pool. I thought it sounded like fun, so I quickly changed my clothes and we drove off to the bar. I enjoyed spending time with Grandpa; he was very easy- going with me and even let me smoke a cigarette from time to time. After we arrived at the bar and Grandpa ordered us some drinks, we went into an isolated room in the back of the bar where a pool table was located and we began to play. Somewhere in the middle of our first game, I looked up to see a large American Indian man with long black hair standing in a dimly lit corner watching us. He looked like he was at least as tall as my dad's brother Sam, my favorite uncle who taught me how to play basketball, who stood six feet, four inches tall. After Grandpa and I finished our second game, the man approached us asking if he could play the winner of the next game. Grandpa calmly responded saying, "Shawn, you go ahead and play him while I go get another beer." After I hesitantly agreed, I was soon left alone in the back room of the bar with this large, strange man who began to rack the balls for me to break.

Near the end of our game, with a stoic look on his face, he calmly said, "You're a really good looking young man; how 'bout you wet my daughter upstairs? She's 19 and never been with a man. I want you to be her first."

As soon as he said that, I instantly recalled having seen a young girl with long black hair sitting on the staircase on the side of the building as we were coming in. "That's all right; I'm fine," I swiftly responded, trying to avoid eye contact while attempting to cruise past his offer and return the focus to the game.

"No! You wet my daughter!" he insisted, raising his voice.

Suddenly my mind began to race, and I asked myself, *"Where is Grandpa? Why hasn't he come back?"* The man's big, intimidating frame started to slowly move towards to me, as I began to walk in the opposite direction around the table. After a few minutes of following me, he began to aggressively chase me back and forth like a grizzly bear stalking its prey. I kept telling him to leave me alone and get away from me, but he persisted. Somewhere in the chase I managed to get away, running out of the secluded back room and into the front the bar where Grandpa sat on a barstool drinking his beer.

When I told him what had happened, he laughed, saying, "I don't knooow, you might like her."

Wondering whether Grandpa had pre-arranged this, and still locked in flight-or-fight mode from my encounter with the wild Indian, I called Dad from a pay phone to come and get me, and waited outside in front of the bar until he picked me up. Grandpa Josef obviously believed that the rite of passage into manhood was found in the bosom of a woman. I was only twelve, but I already knew I wanted nothing to do with that.

In a new school, with new bullies and new trauma, my life in Michigan with Dad was anything but peaceful. Dad's girlfriend Kelley was very strong willed and would often stand up and talk back to him when they were fighting. Her black eyes and busted lips clearly bore the evidence that she was no match for Dad's iron fist. In many ways, Dad was still a child himself, and he didn't seem to know anything about being a father—not that I had any clear idea of what a real father was anyway.

I missed my grandmother back in Ohio something terrible. Without her in my life, I felt more lost and alone than ever. When she told me over the phone that she was divorcing Grandpa Roy for cheating and would be moving in with Mom and Jed, I decided to move back to Ohio to be with her.

Somehow, I never lost hope that things could be different.

CHAPTER 6

—— ☙ ——

"COME ON DILLAN, you can make it!" I shouted.

"Yeah, Dillan, come on!" yelled Lisa and Joe, as the old red tractor slowly started to move.

Dillan's concern that he might miss out on the evening's coveted hay-ride was replaced by a smile as he freely ran and jumped onto the straw-packed flatbed trailer. The youth group cheered as Dolly's husband Carl drove us around the designated winding path through the harvested corn fields, circling the large wooded area on the edge of their spacious property. Laughing and singing, we huddled together to keep warm on the cool fall night of our youth group's harvest party.

Originally invited by a schoolmate, I soon became active in this small Presbyterian youth group. It was far from the lively environment of "holy rollers" at the little white church I'd attended previously, but was considerably less legalistic and judgmental.

As the hayride ended, Dolly and her blonde ponytailed little girl received us with smiles at the back of their large ranch-style house. Dolly was a longstanding member of the old Presbyterian church where she faithfully played piano and attended with her two children Kylie and Macy. Macy and I were the same age and flirted with the idea of "going together"; it lasted for all of two weeks.

"Come inside and warm up. I have some hot chocolate and cookies waiting for you!" said Dolly. Making a beeline through the back door of the house, we filled our bellies with hot chocolate and home-baked treats, and warmed our cold hands by the heat of the wood-burning stove.

Anticipation filled the room as we congregated around the large TV in the den to watch video clips from our previous sleepover at the church, which raised money for hungry children in Africa. Laughter exploded within minutes as we watched Spencer, the comedian in the group, turn on his charm for the camera with funny faces and hand gestures and as pretty, petite Ellen smiled modestly, quickly covering her face with her hands. When the youth director's video camera slowly moved in my direction, my laughter abruptly faded. For the first time, I could see myself. I saw clearly my feminine mannerisms and facial expressions, which were more pronounced during my unrestrained boisterous laugh. I was horrified! From that night on, I made an inner vow that I would work hard to wipe out every socially unacceptable trait. I started with the laughter. As an instinctual actor, I learned through constant observation and study how to perfectly play the role that my inner homophobic critic had assigned. The problem with it all: I lost myself in the editing process.

Rushing adrenalin carried me like a river to the small wooden stage positioned directly in the center of my high school gymnasium. Although the lights were dimmed, I could hear the restless crowd waiting to hear the only freshman soloist chosen to sing for "Panorama," my school's popular annual variety show. The luxury of being a frequent soloist in Miss Kelly's class and singing for my eighth-grade homecoming dance had prepared me for this moment. Gripping the mic ever so tightly to still my quivering hands, I took in a long deep breath--and sang! I sang the Billy Joel song "Just the Way You Are" as if my life depended on it, with all the passion and emotion that I could render. As the song came to an end, I raised my left hand for dramatic effect just I had done in my private bedroom concerts with my sister as a kid, and belted out the last note. My hometown crowd jumped to its feet, cheering and whistling. I'd never experienced such an overwhelming feeling of appreciation and accomplishment. I was hooked!

Attending a high school with one of the top music and drama programs in the state of Ohio afforded me some amazing opportunities to develop my talents. I eagerly jumped into everything I possibly could: I played clarinet in the marching band, symphonic band, and orchestra; I sang in the concert choir, the show choir, and the Ohio Wesleyan honors choir; I was active in the drama club, the radio club, the newspaper sales staff, fall musicals, spring plays, and two community theater organizations. My sophomore year, with several of my classmates, I also started a band which performed at fairs, festivals, and special events. I couldn't get enough.

High school introduced me to a whole new world—a world of new faces, new experiences, and new possibilities. I found new acceptance and connection among the singers, actors, and musicians; I found a place to belong. More than anything, it gave me hope. It embedded within me the idea that I could change the direction of my life, and forge a new path for myself.

Shawn Alex Nemeth

"All right, choir; it's time to get started! Put your books under your seats, sit up nice and tall, and sing from your diaphragm."

Inspiration and admiration took on an entirely new meaning the first time I heard the beautiful singing voice of my high school choir director. His ability to flow seamlessly from his chest voice into an equally developed falsetto created the illusion that his vocal range had no end. Multitalented, he was a skilled dancer, musician, and teacher with the rare ability to infuse passion, kindness, and excellence into his craft. He was tall, lean, handsome, well groomed, and consistently sported a big smile; he embodied class. I wanted to be just like him. Those of us who had the honor of working closely with him affectionately called him "Mr. Hof."

As the lunch bell rang, I grabbed my books, jumped to my feet, and quickly navigated the busy school hallways to the crowded lunchroom. Inside this breeding ground for so much pain and bullying I'd experienced in middle school, anxiety instantly took me by the hand each time I stepped into the loud lunchroom environment. Nervously reaching into my pocket to retrieve the signed lunch pass I'd scored from Mr. Hof that morning, I eagerly handed it to the stressed-out teacher on duty and hurriedly made my way to the safety of the music department practice rooms.

Passing by Mr. Hof's open office door, I stuck my head in and said, "Hi, Mr. Hof!"

"Hi, Shawn," he said, smiling. "How's that Italian aria that you've chosen to sing for solo and ensemble competition coming?" he asked.

"I've been working on it with Helen [my voice teacher], but it still needs a lot of work," I replied with a smirk.

72

"It's a Class A piece; they're not easy, but I know you can do it," he said reassuringly. "I have some time available now if you would like to work on it."

"Thank you; that would be great!" I said appreciatively.

As I pulled my Italian aria book out of my blue nylon bag and placed it upon the upright piano, Mr. Hof turned to me and said, "Shawn, before we get started, I just wanted to tell you how much I appreciate the way you always give one hundred percent of yourself during choir practice. I wish I had a choir room full of people just like you!"

Little did he know, giving my full attention and focus during choir rehearsals was easy for me. When I learned of his personal dream to receive a superior rating at the state choir competition, it became my dream, too. It was a small way to give back to the one who had given me so much.

Mr. Hof was the first man in my life who had taken a genuine positive interest in me. I respected him like no other. I felt consistently encouraged and valued by this humble role model, mentor, and trusted friend. He changed my outlook on life dramatically, all because he believed in me.

The standing ovation at "Panorama" and the superior ratings I received at several science fairs and solo and ensemble competitions had a far greater effect on me than temporarily making me feel good. More important, Mom and Jed noticed me. Feeling a part of *their* family was something that I'd fantasized about while lying in bed in the dark for so many years. I couldn't restrain the all-consuming smile from completely taking my face hostage as I heard them bragging about me a time or two to their friends. *"Maybe NOW things will change,"* I thought. *"Maybe now they will love me."*

By the time I was in high school, Mom had worked her way up into a notable management position at a major department store in Marion. The town newspaper had even written an article about her, celebrating her management and customer-service skills. Like my biological father, my mother possessed a very strong work ethic. With the salary she received from the department store and the monthly back child support payments from suing my father, I was able to take weekly voice lessons, participate in my many extracurricular activities, and dress well for school. Even though I often felt angry that my Mom was never around to protect me from Jed, I highly respected the fact that she alone provided for our family. I scarcely remember Jed working. He mostly partied—at my mother's expense. Hearing him joking about how well he had it made while getting high with his deadbeat buddies made me despise him all the more.

Some of the most valuable life lessons I learned in high school derived from my involvement in the arts. The various challenges I encountered taught me commitment, perseverance, loyalty, and the great difference that passion-infused creativity can generate.

During my freshman year, marching in the band proved downright painful! Like a tired Catholic priest ready for retirement, our director was cold, moody, boring, and uninspiring. As a result, we didn't perform well. Instead of an uplifting force of entertainment, our undeniable incompetence was often the brunt of jokes and ridicule at the football games where we played. The laughter I endured playing the "girly" clarinet provided sufficient embarrassment; I didn't need or want the further humiliation of being part of a subpar band.

My dad's girlfriend had given me the clarinet when I was in seventh grade and strongly encouraged me to join the band to learn how to play it. I would have chosen the saxophone, but I suppose the clarinet had chosen me. I saw several students quit marching band over the course of my freshman year, but I decided to stick it out. Things spiraled from bad to worse when our director decided to enter us into a marching-band competition. He said it was for our experience, but it completely shattered any remaining confidence and morale we had left. At the end of the school year, we were greatly relieved to hear that he'd resigned.

Our new band director came onto the scene as the direct antithesis of our previous leader: always smiling and continually inspiring. With his collegiate experience, he knew exactly how to get things done. In our first meeting, he presented his new vision with handouts, blackboard diagrams, and a motivational speech that breathed new life into our defeated hearts. He told us over and over we could be great, and we grew to believe him.

An extraordinary transformation of our band followed. Over the next three years, our marching band grew from one hundred to three hundred members, and famously became the main attraction at our home football games. We traveled to play in the Cotton Bowl, the Peach Bowl, the Gator Bowl, and at Disneyland, scoring highly in competitions throughout the country. By the time I was a senior, our band ranked eleventh out of more than three hundred high-school marching bands in the entire nation.

Being in the band had become cool, and that girly clarinet I played? Perspective was completely rerouted when I received an award for "Most Improved Musician" in my senior year. I guess the clarinet did choose me.

I wasn't particularly drawn to Henry when we first met. He was a chubby, unattractive, socially awkward, giant-sized teenager who played the piccolo in marching band. He stood out. I had too much baggage of my own to deal with than to be hanging out with piccolo-playing giants, but he made me laugh, and his unexpected wit and kindness drew me in.

Over time, we became good friends and I would occasionally stay the night at his house. Henry's family lived in a nice split-level house with a pool. Half of the entire basement was Henry's room and the other half was storage. Along with a sofa, large TV, computer, and piano, it provided the perfect hangout for two teenage band geeks.

Henry's mom Stella, with her short bleached-blonde hair and distinct masculine walk, was a bus driver at our high school. Her nerdy, detached, often absentee husband Sherman worked for the US Postal Service. Together they made a comfortable living in our small Ohio town. Henry's younger brother Wilbur was a very strange, socially underdeveloped hypochondriac who stayed home from school most of the time, watching TV with his two little dogs. Henry and Wilbur were both obsessed with *Star Wars*. They incessantly watched all the movies and even turned the third bedroom on the main floor of the house into a museum to display all of their memorabilia. Personally, I found little interest in any of it.

This family was a very odd bunch, indeed, but I had fun with them, and their home provided me a safe place to retreat from the escalating chaos at my house.

Abruptly shaken out of sleep by the thunder of heated voices, this Saturday night was no different from many others. I customarily pulled the pillow out from under me and wrapped it around my head, covering both ears to buffer the yelling. I knew the drill; experience told me there was nothing I could do when Mom and Jed were fighting. I must have dozed off again for a short time before I heard smashing glass and my mother screaming. I jumped out of bed, ran down the stairs, and leaped onto Jed's back, attempting to pull him off my crying mother, whom he had pinned against the wall. Grabbing both of my legs, he violently swung me around, throwing me over the coffee table. Before I could fully stand, he jumped on top of me, pulling both arms behind me until I screamed from the pain. "Who do you think you are, little fucker? I'll kill you!" he said.

After dropping my arms and ruthlessly slapping me in the back of the head, he stood up. I wasted no time, seizing the opportunity to leverage my legs up under me, standing back up, and sprinting up the stairs. My heart was racing so fast it was hard to concentrate. Obsessed with the need to protect my mother, I made my way back down the stairs with the hunting rifle my dad had given me in one hand, and a bullet I'd hidden under my mattress in the other.

Reaching the bottom of the stairs, I could see Jed with a cold, murderous look shaking my mother violently, with both of his large hands wrapped around her head. "You bitch," he said. "You'll never get away from me!"

With my hands trembling, trying rapidly to load the gun, I pointed it at Jed and said, "Let her go." His failed response prompted me to raise my voice and say it again, "I said, LET HER GO!"

When Jed saw the gun, he pushed my crying mother to the ground; with a cocky look on his face, he turned to me, holding out both hands. "What are you gonna do, little prick? You gonna shoot me?!" he sarcastically said, smiling. "Come on, shoot me!"

"No, Shawn!" pleaded my Mom. "Don't do it!"

"Shoot me!" he insisted. "Come on you little sissy, shoot me!"

Everything within me wanted to pull the trigger. I hated him. I hated him and I wanted him gone from our lives. But seeing my mother lying there sobbing, begging, and pleading with me not to do it arrested my heart. I threw the gun down, walked out the front door, and ran.

I ran all the way to Henry's house alone in the dark, and sat on their front steps until the sun rose.

Depression had walked with me for many years during my childhood and adolescent years, but during my sophomore year of high school its presence became undeniable to those around me.

"Shawn, I'm so concerned about you," said Mr. Hof. "You used to light up the room every time you entered, but something has happened. I can see you are hurting; something is deeply troubling you. Are you able to talk with me about it? I want to help you if you'll let me."

Caught between fear and anxiety, trust steadied my trembling hand as I did my best to open up and share some of my hidden pain with my caring mentor. Through his guidance, I went to speak with the school's guidance counselor, who contacted my mom, urging that we see a family therapist immediately. By the following week, we ended up at a family counseling center. The therapist decided the best course of action was to meet with us individually before collectively as a family. However, the therapy came abruptly to an end when Jed verbally threatened and threw a chair at the therapist during his private session. Noticing Jed steamrolling out the front door, my mom frantically grabbed my arm as we quickly made our way out to the car. I could feel the fear instantly take hold of my heart. I knew what was coming. Sitting in the back of the car, my hands dug into the black leather seat as Jed raced down the street in a heated rage. By the time he reached the third stop light, my frazzled nerves could take no more. I jumped out of the car and took off running.

Once again, I stayed the night at Henry's and spent several hours talking to his mom Stella about what had happened. Her kindness and sweetness reminded me of my grandmother when I was young, as she consoled me, inviting me to come and live with them. "Really?!" I said. "Do you really mean it?!"

"I do," she said with a smile, reassuringly patting my hand.

Before I called my Mom for permission to move out, I contacted social services concerning my rights. They informed me that I could file charges against her and Jed for child abuse. When I called Mom to ask permission, she exploded in anger saying, "Absolutely not! What would people think?!"

"Mom, the choice is yours," I said, "You either let me move out or I file charges for child abuse."

Angrily, she raised her voice saying, "Who do you think you are?!"

I said, "I contacted social services, Mom. I know my rights."

The tone in her voice instantly changed to sadness as she responded "Shawn, why would you do this to me?"

Henry and I made arrangements to collect my things the following Monday afternoon when Mom and Jed were gone. Loading my last box of things into Henry's car, I felt a trickle of hope return to my deflated heart as we quickly drove away.

I don't recall exactly when the period of serenity ended at Henry's house, but when it did, it came abruptly. Stella, the sweet, caring soul who had drawn me in with her empathetic expression of kindness and mercy, was a modern manifestation of Jekyll and Hyde. The violent tornado that raged within her forged a deep path of destruction when it was unleashed without warning.

The first time I heard her explode in anger, screaming and cursing at the top of her voice, mercilessly slapping and punching her husband, it sent a terrifying shock to the depth of my soul. Continuing her rant, she screamed through the floor at Henry and me in the basement, throwing things down the stairs and hitting our bedroom door like a wild animal freed from its confinement. Deeply frightened and dismayed, I laid face down on my bed, pulling my arms up under me for a sense of protection and comfort. I couldn't move or respond for a time; I felt deceived, betrayed. It was incredibly difficult for me to process. *"I moved out of one house of horrors into another!"* I thought.

"How can this be happening to me?" While lying on my tear-soaked pillow, I felt the stress of my heightened emotions taking over, and I fell asleep just to escape.

I'd never known a woman to be such a violent aggressor and it was extremely troubling for me to witness. I saw Stella beating on Sherman and Henry many times. They both responded the same way, saying and doing nothing. She was tiny in comparison and Henry could have crushed her with one strike, but he didn't. I only saw him grab her hand a time or two to protect himself from her repeated blows to his head. Henry's temperament was more like his dad's: laid back and quiet. Sherman was kind to me and often took us to church on Sundays. I don't recall that Stella ever joined us. Sherman would sometimes wear a tie and jacket when going out to events, while Stella wore jeans and sweatshirts. They couldn't have been any more different from each other. It was fairly easy to see why Sherman was gone so much of the time; when he was home, Stella would constantly shame and put him down. I often thought how I would leave her if she were my wife.

Henry and I never discussed his mother's obvious mental illness. We tried our best to dismiss it, even though it became more recognizable and her outbursts more hurtful. For a short time, we stayed close friends. It was really nice having someone to talk to each day, and Henry was so complimentary of me. I was so needy for acceptance and affirmation that I fed on his every word.

However, things began to take a twisted turn with Henry, too. He began telling me how attractive I was and how fascinated he was with my feet. He began to proposition me, offering me money to massage my feet. I laughed the first time he suggested it, but he kept pursuing me and his continued advances started to feel very uncomfortable. It must have been the combination of needing money to buy a new shirt for show choir and Henry raising the amount of his offer from fifteen to twenty-five dollars which caused me to finally give in. As he began to ardently rub my feet, I did what I had done so many times in my childhood: I checked out. I traveled in my head to the woods next to my grandmother's house and hid behind an old oak tree. When Henry was finished, I felt dirty, mad at myself, determined to never do it again. He said it was only a foot rub; to me, it was selling myself for another's pleasure.

I wish I could say that was the only time, but it wasn't.

Nor was Stella the only bully in the family. Henry's younger brother Wilbur shared his mother's malicious behavior, but in a much more sinister way. I never understood why he turned on me the way he did, but he seemed to get off on it. Daily, I had to walk up the stairs from our basement bedroom to the main floor kitchen to eat. I would often encounter Wilbur sitting on the sofa peering at me with a devious look around the side of the vicious little lap dog he held dangling in front of his face. I could hear him mumbling each time to his dog before setting him free to attack me. I had to clean the blood off my legs several times from these incidents. I was too afraid to make a big deal about it. Where would I go? I would be lying if I said I didn't give that little demon dog a swift kick a time or two for attacking me when no one was home. My helplessness did have limits!

Other times, Stella and Wilbur would be sitting on the sofa together and Wilbur would lean over and whisper into Stella's ear while staring at me with a creepy smile. I knew he was turning her against me, but I felt trapped in my circumstance. Eventually, I would wait until late at night when everyone was asleep to sneak upstairs and eat dinner. I was usually starving by then, but it was far better than having to face their dreadful humiliation. I felt so unwanted in their home, just like I did with my own family. Internally, I know I blamed myself.

At every turn, I felt less and less safe in the house with this strange family.

The bathroom that Henry and I shared in the basement protruded into the adjacent walled storage area beside our bedroom. The builder had framed the small bathroom with two-by-fours and simply nailed up thin paneling around the inside of the room to make the walls. One day when I was stumbling to find the light switch in the dark bathroom, I noticed light bleeding in from the storage area through several small holes in the paneling. Turning on the bathroom light, I walked into the storage area, turned off the light that had been left on, and proceeded to look for the holes in the bathroom walls. I felt nauseated when I located the holes and peered through each one. They were perfectly positioned to provide a view of, well, everything. Suddenly, it all made sense: Henry would often go into the storage area when I was in the bathroom. He had even set up a study area in there. I was hurt, sickened, and furious! Henry had selfishly taken from me the one remaining place in that house where I had felt safe.

Improvisation was one of my favorite drama-class exercises, and Corinne was one of my favorite people. With her gleaming brown eyes and infectious smile, she purposely took me by the hand as we slowly exited stage right in character. Before rejoining our class to receive our critiques, we quickly slipped out of our costumes, laughing, and encouragingly hugging each other. While playfully pushing me as we walked to our seats, she whispered in my ear, "Boomer, you crack me up. Where do you come up with this stuff?"

Partially turning to look at her, I shrugged my shoulders with a playful smile. "Boomer" was one of Corinne's nicknames for me because vocal projection was an unquestionable God-given gift. Her other nickname for me was "Sam," adapted from my infatuation with Sam Harris, the "Star Search" celebrity with the golden vocal chords. I obsessively listened to his albums and even lip-synced to his famous version of "Over the Rainbow" for one of our class projects.

The daughter of a gifted choreographer, Corinne was beautiful, outgoing, multitalented, and one of the most popular girls in our high school. She was captain of the cheerleading team, her red-and-black short uniform skirt that she often wore served as a major distraction to most of the highly hormonal teenage boys. With the gaping hole I carried in my badly damaged self-esteem, I often wondered why Corinne liked ME; but she did. Maybe it was because I made her laugh. We laughed about everything! Hearing her contagious laugh was a cathartic wind which temporarily carried me away from my gnawing emotional pain and fears. We also shared a major love for the theater and performing arts, often talking about moving to New York City together after college to pursue our dream of performing on Broadway. Although I was deeply troubled by my sexuality, I was no doubt smitten with Corinne. Her unexpected friendship soothed me in many ways and provided me courage to believe in myself more.

I struggled so much in high school managing my emotions and knew very little about how to calm myself and work through my high anxiety. The breathing exercises I learned in drama class and prayer were all I had to steady my rollercoaster of emotions. Sometimes they worked; other times they didn't. As a result, performing was often like playing emotional Russian roulette. When I performed well, life was a song filled with dancing rhythms and feel-good melodies, but when

I performed poorly, my emotions knocked me down like a boxer's punch. I was often amazed at the ability Corinne had to blow things off when she screwed up and not let it bother her. Her level of self-confidence was completely foreign to me, and although I tried my best to duplicate it outwardly, it was just another performance. I was completely ignorant to the realization that self-confidence is an inside job.

The snow fell lightly that December afternoon as our show choir piled out of the big yellow school bus and hurriedly made our way into the large white-painted brick nursing home. The strong smell of coffee with a subtle overlay of Ben-Gay provided the perfect reminder of who our afternoon audience would be. After a brief bathroom break, we moved into our choreographed positions in the spacious multipurpose room as Mr. Hof led us through a vocal warmup. A few minutes later, a parade of wheelchairs, walkers, and shuffling seniors slowly filled the festively decorated room.

The creative choreography Corinne's mother Mel had successfully drilled into our heads served us well in entertaining our wide-eyed-crowd. Our school was fortunate to have some very gifted singers and dancers, and our popular show choir often showcased the *crème de la crème*. Throughout our show, we could hear some of the funniest remarks coming from several of the colorful geriatric characters in the audience: Crackly comments like, "I can't hearrr, I can't hear!" and "It's too loud! Turn it dooown!" A few times I had to literally clench my teeth to avoid joining a few others and laughing out loud. The comical comment that finally did me in came when I was singing a solo of Nat King Cole's classic, "The Christmas Song." During the musical interlude, a soft-faced lady on the front row, wearing thick glasses and a shimmery red Rudolph sweatshirt, pointed at me and yelled, "You should be on the Johnny Carson shooow!" At that, I had to succumb to my uncontainable laughter.

The spring of my junior year, our school variety show "Panorama" moved from our high school gymnasium to the historic vaudeville Palace Theater downtown. This beautifully restored gem in the center of our small town was where we also did our fall musical each year. I was selected for the third year in a row to perform, singing a solo, a song with my band, and a duet with Corinne. The often unpredictable voice change I was plagued with through my sophomore year had passed, and I felt more comfortable performing again. I loved the stage! It made me feel alive and lifted me from the shadows of mediocrity, abuse, and shame. When I was performing, I was inspired to believe that I could be someone.

All three performances went really well, and Corinne's mother, who had choreographed our duet, praised me after the show. Mel was known for not being easily impressed and had a reputation for being overly strict and demanding. Some of the students called her "dragon lady" and would often joke about her behind her back. I liked her. I liked her BECAUSE she was tough. It was Mel who took me aside during my later high-school years, challenging me on my diva-like behavior. She told me in no uncertain terms that I was better than that. She was the best at what she did and she made ME better. I was fortunate to work with her in many high school and community theater productions. Her persistent words of wisdom have stayed with me for life: "When you're early, you're on time, but when you're on time, you're late!"

Even though Corinne came running up to me back stage after the performance, congratulating me with a kiss, I had mixed emotions that night. She and several of my other friends were about to graduate and travel off to college in the fall. I couldn't imagine life without them.

When I heard the news over the summer that Mr. Hof had entered a doctoral program and would be minimally involved at our high school for my senior year before leaving entirely, I fell apart and cried for days. It felt as though much of my support system had vanished overnight, replaced by new high school bullies and dark bouts of depression.

Returning home to live with my Mom and Jed halfway through my senior year actually helped. The craziness at Henry's house had reached critical mass. My addiction to store-bought caffeine pills to offset my sleepless nights from obsessive worry and fear about my current living conditions, coupled with the sadness and disappointment over my senior year of high school, forced me to make the unthinkable decision of moving back with my abusive family. I consoled myself with the fact that it would only be for a few months before I left for college in the fall. Mom had also convinced Jed that leaving me alone would be the best course of action because of the potential legalities that had previously been discussed. Surprisingly, he complied. Apart from Jed's trying to bribe me to stay quiet about his dealing cocaine out of their master bedroom while Mom was working, everything else remained uneventful between us.

With her large-rimmed glasses, curly brown hair, and frumpy appearance, Helen was just another common face in the crowd. But when she sang, the air in the room stood still. A gifted operatic soprano with the rich, full tone of an alto, Helen was a musical treasure. However, winning an international operatic competition, which provided her the platform to sing in the grandest opera houses of Europe along with numerous opportunities of possible fame, would not deter her from what she deemed her highest calling in life: providing a stable environment for her little boy. As a single mother, Helen knew the cost of pursuing the stage would require her being absent from her son most of the time. She humbly resolved to a life of academia, teaching voice and piano. I had the honor of becoming a direct beneficiary of her loving sacrifice, studying voice with her my junior and senior years of high school.

Helen and Mr. Hof became friends while working on their doctorates at Ohio State University. What a wonderfully strange coincidence when the colorful pieces of the tapestry of our life connect.

The intensity of our concert choir rehearsals took on new form my senior year as Mr. Hof diligently prepared us for the state choir competition. He had seen some amazing talent come and go through the doors of his choir room over the years but his dream of receiving a superior rating at state remained unfulfilled. There were more gifted soloists in years past, but in some strange way the collective sound produced when we lifted our voices in harmony was nothing short of magical. Could this be the year?

For months, Helen had been guiding me through a musical obstacle course of vocal exercises and Italian diction lessons, preparing me for my entry audition as a vocal performance major at Ohio University. No one in my family had gone to college before me. I was terrified. I felt so unprepared to live on my own and face the responsibilities that my new life as a college student would bring. I was far too embarrassed to tell anyone that I didn't even know how to balance a check book.

Corinne insisted on coming home from college for the weekend of my college audition to drive me three hours south to Athens, Ohio, to the School of Music. I was so excited to see her when she arrived early that Saturday morning to pick me up. I missed her far more than I had the ability to express. She had no idea of the value of the gift she was giving me. Her presence alone made me feel better. It took only minutes before we were laughing once again. We laughed and sang the entire way.

Hopes ran high as our high school concert choir eagerly filled each row of the risers that Saturday afternoon at Bowling Green State University for the state choir competition. Though I would never negate the effort poured out by the other choir members that day, nor arrogantly assume that the musical notes which soared from my vocal chords were any better than the rest, it *is* highly probable that few wanted a superior rating more that day than Mr. Hof and I. I say this only because of what that day alone meant to both of us on a deeply personal level. For Mr. Hof, it was the golden seal on the finale of a successful era that he lovingly poured his heart, sweat, and tears into—and a towering new door of opportunity and dreams to be obtained.

For me, it was my final way of honoring and giving back to the choirmaster who had saved my life several years before. We sang. God smiled. We earned a superior rating!

My dismal senior year ended up yielding much fruit in the end with a national choral award, a national speech and drama award, a musical theater award, and recognition in *Who's Who Among American High School Students* for the second year. I was also accepted into the Ohio University School of Music as a vocal performance major and awarded a special talent scholarship.

Not bad for a frightened, long-haired little boy from Chester Street.

CHAPTER 7

———— ϙ ————

SPAIN, WITH ITS spectacular landscapes, grand architecture, and bustling city streets, was a sight to be seen. Andrea translated for me
as I spoke in the largest non-denominational church in the country,
as well as at a Biblical training institute in Madrid. We also spent
several hours in a television studio recording songs in Spanish to be
played on Christian programs throughout Spain and other Spanish-
speaking countries. *Missions Director* was one of the many hats I
wore as an associate pastor in our California-based church. One of
my responsibilities in this role was to travel to the various countries
to meet, evaluate, and encourage the missionaries and organizations
that our congregation supported financially. Before we returned to
the states, we had to make one more trip into a coastal country of
Africa. The single missionary we supported there was a born native, the brother of the head counselor to the king of this influential
nation.

With a doctorate in linguistics, this man's primary responsibility
was to create and teach a written language to one of the isolated
tribes and to eventually translate the Biblical scriptures into that
language. As an undercover Christian, his work was against the law
in this Muslim country and put his life in danger. Any contact we
had with him was generally through specially coded emails and occasional phone calls. Prior to our trip, I had tried for several weeks
to contact him by phone without success. All I had was his physical

address. Andrea and I arrived at the hotel late in the afternoon and spoke with the concierge about hiring a guide. To avoid arousing too much suspicion, we pretended to be tourists. This also gave us time to spend with a guide to see if enough trust could be established before coercing him to lead us to our secret destination the next morning.

In all of our travels, Andrea and I had never felt such fear before. It permeated the city streets and showed on the hopeless faces of the heavily oppressed women. The men were overly aggressive and even offensive at times. As we walked down the crowded street, it was disturbing to see the left side full of men lounging and laughing at cafes and eateries, while the women and children gathered and worked on the right. The stark contrast was nauseating, a picture I will never forget. Our guide was adamant about taking us to several shops in the market area. We found the store clerks abrasive and rude when we declined buying their goods. By the easily observed non-verbal communication being exchanged, it was obvious that we were being played by our guide. He was strategically taking us to the shops of his relatives and close friends. They continued to shout at us that they knew we were from California and must be rich. With a heightened feeling that we could be mugged and robbed if this charade continued, I ordered our guide to take us back to the hotel. He argued, but complied.

The next morning, Andrea and I decided on a different strategy. Fully aware that it could be dangerous, we hired a taxi driver to take us directly to the home address that we had been given for the missionary. We were completely surprised when we arrived at a very spacious and lavish home--not the customary dwelling place of a missionary. Our pleasantly surprised, gracious host greeted us with hugs and kisses. We later learned that because of his brother's high position with the king, the missionary was required to maintain a higher standard of living. As a result, his brother arranged for him this home and a staff. He informed us that over time, his brother had grown suspicious of his questionable activities and warned him that that there would be consequences if he had any more foreign visitors. He had been monitored, which greatly increased his isolation and loneliness. His beautiful home retreat had become his confinement. He was so humbled and appreciative that we took the risk to come in spite of all the obstacles that stood in our way.

During our visit, we had an insightful time of communion, conversation, and observation of the work and future plans of this remarkable man. Before we left, he honored us by having his cook prepare the most decadent meal that would rival the finest restaurants in New York and Los Angeles. It was a culinary experience that yielded unfamiliar delight to the palate, all with an air of refined contentment. As we tearfully said our goodbyes to this generous soul, we knew that our lives had been forever enriched.

If the South American mission-field bliss was the original birthplace of the marital deception I surrendered to, our trip to Spain and Africa became the shattering mirror of reality. Contention moved in with us and became a permanent part of our marriage. We agreed on nothing and constantly challenged each other. It became painfully apparent that Andrea and I didn't even seem to share many of the same values. To me, ministry was about people: the giving of oneself to build them up and meet their needs. It was about leading out of relationship instead of out of position and title. Andrea and I sharply disagreed on this leadership philosophy, and it continued to be a source of agitation in all of our years of working together in ministry.

When the senior pastor became aware of our marital problems, he insisted that we meet with him on a weekly basis for counseling. I found this incredibly uncomfortable and even unprofessional at times because I worked with him, and he and his wife were so close to Andrea. Even so, he was a masterful counselor and provided strategic guidance during the time that he advised us. He told me privately that my wife had learned how to manipulate and control me. He assured me that if I didn't get a handle on it, she would run my life. How insightful! This was my constant battle throughout our turbulent four-year marriage.

The day I said my marriage vows and made my commitment, I purposed in my heart to stay true to my word, regardless of the circumstances or how I felt. I honestly wanted to do my best to be a good husband. Every day, I prayed that God would give me unconditional love and passion for my wife; that I would desire her sexually and would want to be with her. Divorce was not an option for me. If God chose during the ceremony to not remove from me the same-sex desires that lived in me, then I would continue to pray and trust until He did. I had to. My very survival depended on it. I held onto every word of the biblical promises even more than before. I had been taught that being gay was a sin and an abomination to God. I was also taught and believed that God was loving and faithful. Why would a loving and faithful God refuse to change me and then condemn me for being a way that I never wanted to be in the first place?

In the midst of such blinding delusion, controversy, and conflict, the one thing that can never be taken from me is the genuineness of my heart, faith, and tears.

Late one afternoon, I came home from my office to find Andrea crying on the sofa. When I asked her what was wrong, she said, "I feel lost. I miss being in leadership."

In my previous negotiations for employment with the governing board of the California church, it was made clear that I would be the only one in a pastoral role. They believed it to be the best thing for the church as well as for us in our first year of marriage. Knowing my fiancée's ministry background, they wanted us to be sure that she would be willing and content with this agreement before I made my decision to take their offer. In our discussions, Andrea seemed really excited about making the change. She expressed that being able to break from the stresses of leadership would be a welcome benefit for her. She claimed that she wanted to focus her efforts on building our home and starting a family. I believed it to be what she wanted.

Then, with her eyes tightly closed, Andrea held my hands tightly and forced out the words, "Shawn, I don't know how to tell you this because I know how important it is to you: I don't want to have children. I know I said that I did, but I guess I want my career more." There was no hiding the apparent shock on my face. I felt like I had been kicked in the gut. I was so clear in our pre- and post-engagement discussions about my longing to be a father and to raise children with the brand of love and parenting that I'd never experienced for myself. With an apparent heartfelt sincerity and conviction, she had said that she wanted the same. In my fragile attempt to keep the issue on the table, I earnestly tried to console her with the proposition that we could wait a few years and maybe she would feel differently. By the look on her face, I knew that she wouldn't.

After some time had passed, the institute in Dallas where Andrea and I had met several years before contacted me about a new position, to join the faculty as the director of their traveling band and vocal group. They also wanted to hire Andrea part-time as the assistant director. This musical group had at one time been the shining jewel of the institute and the primary marketing and public relations team. It had a long, successful history in producing powerful praise-and-worship re-cordings and notable Christian songwriters and performers. However, the group's days of glory and influence were long gone. This outdated singing group had devolved into a mere shadow of what it had once been, and an increasing embarrassment to the institute. Initially, I wasn't the least bit interested in taking on this sinking ship. The direc-tor of the institute told me that he trusted implicitly my artistic abilities and that I had *carte blanche* as far as he was concerned. "You can make the group into anything you want and I will back you complete-ly," he promised. Although his words enticed me and the challenge sounded appealing, with our undeniably mounting marital problems, I knew that it could be personally disastrous for Andrea and me.

To counter the Dallas offer, I gained a raise in salary to stay in my cur-rent position at the California church, as well as the incredible opportu-nity to eventually pioneer a separate congregation of my own. Having previously expressed to me her desire to co-lead a church with me in the future, Andrea suddenly wanted nothing to do with this. Deep in my heart, I knew that staying was the most logical fit for us, because the current church provided the needed buffer for Andrea and me to coexist. However, she obviously saw that buffer as her enemy.

There was no denying that unconsciously, Andrea and I both des-perately wanted to be something that we were not. I wanted to be straight and Andrea wanted to be a man--or at least, she wanted the titles and positions in ministry that were typically afforded men. What a hollow life we were leading, far removed from the true purpose of selfless, life-affirming ministry.

CHAPTER 8

———— ৎ৳ ————

Twice during my eight-hour recovery room battle, death came close to claiming its prize, which made my pre-surgical premonition appear to be much more than a hallucination induced by too much anesthesia. Waking up alone in intensive care hours later with stabbing pain from the breathing tubes in my throat and from the deep incision in my abdomen, I wondered if death might have been the better option. I'm forever grateful that my merciful Maker had other plans for me.

Andrea came to visit me a few hours later in ICU, informing me that the Dallas hospital had failed to communicate anything to her about my close-to-death experience. Aware that a general recovery-room timeframe was under three hours, she approached the nurses' station multiple times for information but received none. Only when a doctor approached her eight hours after my surgery to inform her that they were moving me into the intensive care unit did Andrea realize the full extent of my condition. The medical profession defines what happened to me as pulmonary edema. I was basically drowning in my own body fluids, probably from an allergic reaction to the anesthesia. Adding to my distress, my intestines temporarily shut down, rendering me unable to relieve myself. The pain I experienced as a result was far greater than the chronic back pain that had initially driven me to have the lumbar spinal fusion.

Andrea and I had decided that I would have the much-needed surgery at the end of the semester, thinking that it would grant me adequate time to heal and recover during our extended holiday breaks. As a result of fulfilling both of our class examination responsibilities, Andrea was unable to spend much time at the hospital. I was completely unprepared for how being alone in the hospital in such a vulnerable and fragile state would trigger my childhood feelings of abandonment and abuse. I said nothing to Andrea because of her heavy workload, but I desperately wanted her to stay by my side.

Since my early childhood, I had suffered with neck and back pain. It wasn't until I was a young adult that I'd discovered that I had been born with a minor spinal birth defect. My parents never seemed to believe me when I complained about the pain, which most likely contributed to why it was left untreated. Because my back issues had not been properly diagnosed, I repeatedly suffered throughout my teen and early adult years by doing chores and activities that my spine was incapable of performing safely.

In my twenties, while driving to work at my first church position in southern Illinois one rainy night, my accumulating back problems went over the edge when my car was broadsided by an oncoming vehicle. Treated for whiplash and a cervical spine injury, I was unable to work for months. When I was able to return to my responsibilities at the church, I had to quickly retreat to a room adjacent to the sanctuary to lie flat on my back frequently during my workdays. I spent months going to chiropractic appointments and living with debilitating pain. Over time, I was able to return to my everyday routine, but the chronic pain and the acute sciatica which eventually developed dominated my life.

By the third year of my marriage, my pain was literally paralyzing at times. I recall many nights having to depend on Andrea to help me to bed because of the pain and temporary loss of mobility in my left leg.

It became increasingly challenging not to allow the fear of becoming physically disabled to completely submerse me in discouragement. Following the surgery, as I completed the fifth and final physical therapy session that my limited insurance plan provided me, it was quite obvious that I would have to take my rehabilitation into my own hands. Still walking with a cane and unable to tie my own shoes, I hobbled out to the college running track night after night to walk my laps. My slow, feeble movements resembled those of someone much older, but each persistent step I took filled me with an inner strength and hope that I would not always be like this. Something far greater inside me would not allow me to give up.

While my back continued to heal, a bed was installed in the back of our tour bus so that I could rest as needed during our rigorous traveling schedule. Sitting for long periods of time was still too agonizing for me, but lying flat helped diminish the pain. My inability to participate in transporting the equipment back and forth from our bus had long been a source of emotional discomfort for me. I never wanted any of the team to feel like I was pulling rank or taking advantage of them. Now, following my surgery, I was incapable of even lifting my own suitcase for many months and had to rely on a student to see my bags to our hotel room each night. I found this incredibly humiliating. There were days that I struggled to get out of bed because of the intense pain and looming depression, but I persistently summoned the stubbornness that I'd inherited from my mother to press forward, determined to get to the other side.

As I fought for months to regain what I had lost, I was often humbly reminded of the times that I had been so impatient at the mall or in the line at the grocery store when I encountered the disabilities of others. How insensitive and un-Christlike I had been. "Never again," I promised myself.

It's amazing how the depth and insight of spiritual teaching becomes so much clearer when we are walking through the darkness. Much more than our victories, pain makes us who we are.

As soon as Andrea and I walked through the double glass doors of the large chain bookstore on that brisk, windy Saturday afternoon, I smelled the comforting aroma of coffee brewing. The big, colorful tables near the front of the store with their eye-catching displays welcomed us with a warm embrace. We both loved it here! We could easily spend hours curiously pulling books from the shelves like fine hidden treasures to be admired and studied. Our shared passion for learning was one of the highlights of our relationship, and we found abundant pleasure in sharing and listening to the discoveries of one another's research. Our general custom when first arriving at the bookstore was to separate for a period of time while we collected our stack of bounty to bring back to the wooden study table we shared.

While casually walking past an aisle I had not been down before, I observed something that was about to redirect my life path. Prominently labeled in bold white letters was a section called "Gay and Lesbian." At first, I quickly turned away and walked farther down the aisle, afraid that someone might recognize me and see me staring at the taboo topic. Worse yet, what if Andrea saw me?! But I couldn't resist. I had to walk down there one more time to get a better look. "How large is this section?" I asked myself. It seemed to house hundreds of books. I had always assumed that gay writings were generally erotic and pornographic; that's what I had been taught. However, to my surprise, I found a much broader selection of reading material.

Driving home that evening, I felt completely enticed, yet profoundly confused. In the days that followed, I tried my best to stay away from that bookstore and forget what I had seen. I couldn't. One Friday afternoon while Andrea was teaching, I went back to that same bookstore. What was I looking for? I didn't know for sure. Was it information? Arousal? Maybe both. One thing I knew for certain: I had an overwhelming curiosity to learn more. I returned to the bookstore many more times, my strategy always the same: I would select a larger book or two on subjects that I would be expected to have in hand—books like history, theology, and self-help. Then I would slowly wander down the aisle of my burning curiosity and stand in the adjacent section. I would quickly glance over into the forbidden land, scanning until a title caught my attention. After looking both ways to ensure that no one was coming, I would snatch a book off the shelf and place it behind the others. Finding a secluded spot in the store, usually in a single corner chair, I would then place the forbidden book inside the larger one. This created the perfect shield as my inquisitive mind visited a strange and fascinating world that I had never known existed. There were travel books, poetry books, biographies, even a book recognizing internationally famous and successful people throughout history who were gay.

Of course, there were also books about the tragedies of gay people, but what I found most compelling were the many stories of others living open, successful, and fulfilling lives, happy with themselves—not hiding and suffering in silence like I was.

There was something in the deepest part of me that wished that I could be part of the world that existed in the pages of those books, but it seemed completely unattainable for me. I was taught that if I acted on my desires, I would die of disease and move so far away from God that I might never find my way back. That terrified me.

One of the many perks of being a faculty member at the training institute was a personal key to the Olympic-size indoor pool. Often, when the pool was officially closed, I would leave my office and spend an hour or so swimming and doing water-resistant exercises to strengthen my back. Over time, our band had become quite accustomed to my regular swimming routine. Karl, one of the singers who traveled with us, stopped by my office one afternoon to ask if he could join me for my evening swim. "Sure," I said, thinking that his company would be a nice variation to my daily discipline.

Karl was a kind, handsome, athletic guy with brown hair, striking blue eyes, and a tall, chiseled frame. Being one who exercised consistently himself, Karl had expressed to me that I had good genetics and encouraged me to further develop my naturally lean body.

Every time I entered the pool area, the strong smell of chlorine reminded me of swimming at the YMCA during my elementary school years. Even though the sizable pool was heated, it was still cool enough to shock our nervous system when Karl and I dived in. After an hour or so of swimming laps, Karl asked me if we could sit in the Jacuzzi for a bit before leaving. Since that was my usual custom, I readily agreed.

As I stepped into the hot tub, my body instantly melted into the invigorating, healing waters. I laid my head back, closed my eyes, and relaxed as the pressure from the water jets massaged and rejuvenated my tired muscles. Karl sighed deeply, expressing how terrific it felt as he entered the opposite side of the Jacuzzi. After a short period of silence in our steamy retreat, I could feel that Karl was staring at me. I had often pondered Karl's seemingly flirtatious behavior, but always passed it off to my imagination.

As I looked up, he quickly turned away, realizing he had been caught; but the frantic, awkward darting of his eyes in various directions made him even more obvious. Suddenly, I knew that my intuition about Karl's attraction to me had been accurate. Anxiety began to rush over me as my heart rate elevated and arousal saturated my body. I clumsily left, avoiding any eye contact with Karl and trying my best to act normally. However, my brain chemistry was obviously not ready to let go, as sensual and erotic scenes of Karl and me together dominated my dreams that night.

The entire next day, I waffled between excitement and shame as though my dreams had been real, and that I had somehow participated in something morally and spiritually forbidden. I beat myself up for the arousal I experienced. I prayed as I had done countless times before that God remove any impure thoughts and protect my dreams as I slept at night. It didn't help much. Something deep inside me had been awakened and I couldn't seem to shake it.

The day before our band was about to leave for a ten-day tour, I made an impromptu evening visit to the men's dormitory. I wanted to see how our group members had fared on their semester exams, and make certain that they were packed and ready to go. By that time, most of the other students had left for spring break; the usually bustling high-rise, which had at one time been a hotel, was mostly vacant. I moved through my student checklist fairly quickly, since several of our guys shared rooms. When I first arrived at the dormitory, I knocked on Karl's door, but he wasn't in. I thought I would try once more before calling it a night. After I knocked three or four times, the door opened. Karl, wearing little more than a broad, welcoming smile, invited me in. Throwing his arms up to give me a tight hug, he expressed how glad he was to see me. He calmly informed me that his roommate had already left for break.

I could feel a tantalizing mist of anxiety spray over me as I realized that Karl and I were in his room alone.

Well acquainted with my challenging back issues and recognizing that I was in pain from being up on my feet too long, Karl invited me to lie on his floor to alleviate the pressure. I gladly did so. Propped up on his elbows and seductively lying back on his bed, he confidently said, "I am really good at massages, and if you'll take your shirt off, I would be more than happy to give you one. I know it would make you feel better." I was somewhat stunned by his brazen invitation.

My erotic dreams had only increased my physical attraction to Karl. "There is no doubt that for the moment, it would make me feel better," I thought. Every part of my body wanted to feel his hands on me, but I knew if I allowed him to massage me, it would all be over.

I instantly thought about the founding director of our group who had been fired for having sex with his student. He was a brilliant musician and songwriter who has been called one of the most gifted to have ever served at the institute. He later died of AIDS, humiliated and despised. I didn't want that to be my epitaph.

So, doing what I did best, I quickly moved into survival mode. I playfully brushed off Karl's massage invitation, denied my feelings, and emotionally cut him off. He remained in the group, but I kept a notable distance from him. When he tearfully approached me sometime later to inquire whether he'd done something wrong, I played ignorant. I wasn't adequately equipped to deal with his emotions, because I didn't even know how to constructively analyze and work through my own.

Following one of our most memorable worship events that just happened to have been held at a Florida Bible-training school, I was approached by a successful producer from Nashville. I accepted, mostly out of curiosity, when he asked if he could take Andrea and me out to lunch. As we sat down at the table in the popular Italian restaurant, this bald producer with round-rimmed glasses turned to me directly and asked, "Shawn, what do you want to do? Where do you see your life headed?"

Without hesitation, I answered, "I want to be used by God to change people's lives."

Passionately and sincerely he responded, "There is a very unique and rare anointing on your life, my friend. I would love to help you do that. I can pull together the best musicians in Nashville and help you produce an incredible worship album. All you have to do is say the word."

"Could this really be happening?" I wondered. It was one of my dreams! This man had produced albums for some of the most successful people in the Christian music industry, including an internationally prominent worship leader/song writer from the United Kingdom whom I admired greatly. I sat there stunned, allowing a few moments for his words sink in.

Before I had the opportunity to say much in response, Andrea leaned forward and said, "I write songs, too!"

The screeching brakes of reality brought the vehicle of possibility to a halt.

"If I pursue this opportunity," I thought, *"Andrea will make our already difficult marriage a living hell."*

So I didn't pursue it. I responded the same way when opportunity arose around a new song I had written. It was beginning to draw some notable attention, and I'd been approached by a well-known worship leader who wanted to record it. I never pursued that, either.

As I continued to watch my dreams evaporate, they were replaced by depression, resentment, and despair. It was obvious that the years of constant struggle and stuffed emotions in our marriage were causing me to lose the fire and passion that had always given me my edge. I began to completely shut down. Andrea and I became more distant from each other and I merely went through the motions of our marriage to keep peace.

I felt as though I were an actor playing a role in a staged production to which I had no real-life emotional attachment.

To self-medicate and periodically check out from the emotional pain and turmoil in my life and marriage, I reverted to what I had used in the darkness of my teenage years: porn and masturbation. I had ascertained at a very young age when finding my stepfather's porn collection hidden under his bed that the combination of porn and self-pleasure made me feel better. No matter how bad things were, I could lock myself in my room and momentarily escape from my suffering. It had been traumatically wired into my brain and became my regular self-care regimen.

As I grew up and entered into ministry work, my exposure to porn was minimal, but the masturbation continued. However, the tremendous shame and guilt I experienced from giving in to the only way I knew to release the immense pressure was monumental. I had been taught that *thinking it in your heart* was the same as *doing it*. I found it especially challenging to masturbate without the thinking part, although I was determined to master the craft.

During one of our many ministry trips, I found an unwrapped gay magazine one afternoon at a mainstream bookstore. It was the first time I had ever remembered seeing one. Buying it to accommodate my self-pleasure was a process that quickly escalated into my drug of choice. Buying magazines soon led to renting pornographic videos when my wife was out of town or at a women's function. I would rent only straight porn because of the immense fear I carried of being caught. In my world, both were unacceptable, but a sexual attraction to men was considered unthinkable by most; it was the worst thing imaginable for someone in ministry. I struggled with the same inner turmoil I'd had as a teenager, often on my knees crying buckets of tears and shouting at God, "Why can't I be normal?! It isn't fair that I can't feel any sexual attraction towards women! Please, God, I beg of you, change me!"

Unaware of the complexities of addiction, I would often agonize for days in prayer and self-loathing as to why I didn't seem to have enough self-control. I tried to stop but it only grew worse. I felt my hands shaking like those of a heroin addict as I drove to get my fix at the video store.

Early one Sunday, while Andrea was at home recovering from the flu, I decided to get out of the house to enjoy the beautiful weather. It was one of those rare days in Dallas with the humidity low, winds calm, and the Texas sun just warm enough to warrant a tee shirt and pair of shorts. I drove to a park close to downtown that I had seen but never been to before, and ventured out for a walk. I have always been some-what directionally challenged, but it didn't take long to realize that I must be close to Cedar Springs (the legendary gay area of Dallas) when I saw what appeared to be a gay couple playing volleyball to-gether with their shirts off. Unconsciously, intentionally, or not, I was there! My attention was now firmly frozen in a space between all-out fear and enticing curiosity.

As I walked deeper into the park, I came to an area full of parked cars where the flirtatious and sensual interaction among countless guys was undeniable. I could see a white Jeep out of the corner of my right eye slow down and follow me as I walked along the winding black-topped road. After what seemed like many minutes, I rustled up enough nerve to turn my head and look. I saw a very handsome guy with dark curly hair staring at me. When he saw me look back at him, he smiled. I nervously smiled back. He quickly drove ahead and pulled into a parking spot. My heart began to beat rampantly. *"What is that about?"* I thought. *"Does he want me to go over and talk to him,"* I wondered. I was so out of my comfort zone.

Completely unfamiliar with what came over me, I approached the white Jeep. With a warm friendly smile, the handsome man leaned toward the open passenger window and asked me if I wanted to get in to talk. I did. He said, "This is your first time here, isn't it?"

"Yes", I replied, nervously laughing to release some of the tension.

"I could tell when I saw you walking," he laughed, softly putting his hand on my left knee. "You need to be careful. Cops often come here to flirt and coerce guys to make a move on them so they can ar-rest them."

At hearing this, my heart sank for a moment, but I was too enamored with the attention I was receiving from this cute guy to let it bother me much.

"Would you like to come back to my place for a bit?" he asked calmly.

"I'm not sure," I responded. "I have never done anything like this before."

"I can assure you, I'm a nice guy," he said with a playful smirk. I found his strong confidence and straightforward approach putting me a little more at ease. "See that brick high-rise over there through the trees? I live there on the tenth floor," he said. "We don't have to do anything but just hang out, if that's all you're comfortable with."

I was caught completely off guard as this attractive man confidently shoved my willing body up against the side of the elevator in his residential building to kiss me passionately. As our lips locked, I felt a hot, electrifying sensation spread throughout my body. I had never felt so turned on as I did in that moment. Even though my adulterous behavior was so wrong, it felt so right. When I kissed a girl—and I had kissed many up until the time I was married—it had never felt like this. It always felt like something was off, like it was *unnatural* in some obscure way. Yet, in that one kiss with that man, all my years of agonizing questions and tormenting frustrations simply evaporated.

After we entered his contemporary loft, we talked for only a brief time before all my pent-up years of high-school and college crushes, those endless hours of porn watching and secret fantasies came rushing out of me like the Colorado River.

I told him that it was my first time. He said he didn't believe me.

Stepping into the tour bus after our final concert in Colorado, Andrea suddenly encountered a couple of the band members and me cutting up. My heavy laughter forced out a belch, which made the two guys in front of me laugh even harder. With a firm tone loud enough for everyone to hear, Andrea self-righteously said, "Shawn! WE don't act like that!" The bus quickly became silent. No longer caring what others saw or heard, I turned, looking directly at her and strongly said, "Don't ever TELL me what I can and cannot do!" Shock and surprise glazed over Andrea's face. I was finished with her controlling behavior.

I walked toward the front of the bus, sat down in one of the seats, and put my headphones on. Truth be told, I had been finished for several months. The revelatory elevator kiss had done it for me.

I knew what I had to do, but the thought of leaving my students and ministry killed me inside. There was so much that I loved about my career and life, and in the bigger picture of possibilities, things were just beginning to take off. In just a few months, I would be speaking in Costa Rica as part of a ministry team with one of the top Christian pop groups in the world, and our band had been given the green light to record a live worship album over the upcoming year. As soon as we returned to Dallas from our current tour, Andrea and I were scheduled to fly to Mexico to speak and lead worship at a conference for several thousand people. How could I leave now?

My mind quickly relived a television interview Andrea and I had done just a few days before while on tour. Both of us smiled, laughed, and held hands in front of the camera as though we had such a loving and healthy relationship. A young woman from the audience approached us directly after the interview and commented, "One day I hope to have a wonderfully close marriage like the two of you."

I felt sick inside. I wanted so badly to scream out, "It's a lie! It's ALL a lie!" But I didn't. I smiled and played the part I was expected to play. How could I stand before all those people in Mexico and play the part again? This time, I was done.

That afternoon, while Andrea was out shopping for our next day's trip to Mexico, I quickly packed everything I could fit into my car and drove away. Hot, salty tears fell down my cheeks as I took one last look at my life through the rearview mirror. *"Will I ever get to publicly sing or speak again?"* I wondered. I didn't know for sure. But one thing I did know: I didn't want to live my entire life without finding true love. From that one forbidden Sunday afternoon kiss, I had come to know that I would never find it with a woman.

I left my life to *find* my life.

CHAPTER 9

—— ❡ ——

THE PIERCING MARCH winds reminded me that I was no longer in Texas as I strolled the lively streets of downtown Chicago, with its colorful mélange of personalities, cultures, and examples of creative genius around each new corner. Every step I took breathed fresh life, hope, and promise into my tired soul as I dreamed of what my world could eventually become.

It had taken me four strenuous months of grieving, job hunting, and bunking with friends to get here, but I'd made it. I was living in the Oak Park area in small century-old studio apartment next to the Unity Temple, which was designed by famed architect Frank Lloyd Wright. I no longer had a car or much money to my name, but I didn't care.

I felt as though the Angel of Mercy had stepped into my world and opened the cold, locked iron doors that had secured my lifelong imprisonment. I was free—free to be me. It was so liberating just to know that I was still able to change my life, just as I had done when I had walked to the little white church as boy, and again the day I drove off to college as a young man. I had within me the resilience, capability, and fortitude to determine my path and write my personal story.

There was a small vintage movie theater just down the street from where I lived that I frequented when I had the opportunity. One afternoon on my day off work, I decided to catch a matinee of the newly released *Moulin Rouge*. The love songs that I'd grown up listening to, brilliantly recycled in the movie's soundtrack, took on new meaning as I floated on a romantic cloud of enchantment and possibility. I was so caught up in the beauty of it all that I watched the movie twice. One could say I was experiencing the feelings and excitement of adolescence all over again, now as an out gay man in my early thirties. As a teenager, I'd never felt the freedom to respond to my natural instincts of attraction and desire. The flirting, the holding hands, the butterflies, the carefully folded little notes passed in class when the teacher wasn't looking, the whole dating thing. *"Can this be?"* I wondered. *"Can I actually live a happy life, true to myself and comfortable with who I am?"* It seemed too good to be true, after all my years of dismissing, stuffing, and living in denial.

However, I soon discovered the price of my newfound freedom was extremely costly, much more than I'd ever expected to pay.

Walking away from my ministry career as abruptly as I had was something I would have never considered suggesting that anyone else in my position do. It seemed completely foolish, selfish, and irresponsible. After speaking with a trusted mentor, I arrived at the daunting conclusion that I would have never left if I had talked with Andrea and consulted with my supervising leadership before just walking away. Shame would have dominated as it always had and I would have bowed once more to its power over me.

I knew my abrupt departure must have seemed crazy to most people who believed my marriage to Andrea to be something it wasn't, knowing that only a few who traveled and worked closely with us had witnessed the truth. I had to compartmentalize everything I had been taught, and what I myself had taught, to keep moving forward.

Several months after I'd left, I received an encouraging message through a mutual friend from the person who had worked the closest with Andrea and me. He related how sorry he was for the pain and adjustment I was going through. He also communicated that although he loved us both, he was happy for me that I would no longer be in that rocky marriage. His words meant so much to me, because for months I had felt that people cared more about keeping the "perfect ministry couple" together than about anything else.

In all of the heartfelt conversations and tears I shared with my friends, I never once mentioned my inner turmoil with my sexuality. Although Andrea had made the comment that she needed to "save [me] from [my] homosexuality" during one of our heated telephone discussions, I boldly denied it. The state of my marriage was in shambles sufficient for me to cling to the logic that I needed not to discuss my "gay issue" with anyone as a prominent reason for leaving, and I didn't. I would have left the marriage regardless of my sexuality. My being gay was true, but I'd not yet fully surrendered to the magnitude of how my sexual identity and its associated trauma seeped into every facet of my life, relationships, and decision making.

I would have never married Andrea if I'd unconditionally loved and accepted myself. I was still unwittingly trying to divert attention from what had haunted me all of my life: that I'm gay. It isn't a lifestyle choice or a sexual preference; it's who I am.

I was too afraid that if I told my friends my true reasons for leaving, I would find that just like everyone else in my life, their love would be revealed as conditional. My need to feel safe perpetuated my silence.

As the line of passengers in front of me entered the cramped quarters of the commercial airplane, I politely squeezed in front of the large pear-shaped man sitting in the aisle seat to reach my seat by the window. I'd been waiting for this day for weeks and the mixed bag of anticipation and anxiety I'd been carrying was about to burst. I was flying to Los Angeles to meet Cole for the first time and to accompany him as his date to Elton John's annual Oscar party. I couldn't believe this was happening!

Cole began calling me off the cuff from Dallas only three weeks before after seeing my picture from a guy I'd dated briefly. We seemed to connect uncannily after the first phone call. After talking regularly for a week and a half, he playfully asked one night, "How spontaneous are you?'

"I like spontaneity," I responded (with hidden reservation). "What do you have in mind?"

"What would you think about allowing me to fly you out to Los Angeles to meet me in person?" he asked in a flirtatious tone.

Previously, Cole had expressed that he was particularly interested in me because of my ministry background, knowing that we shared the same religious beliefs. Having not heard this expressed before from another gay guy, I was equally interested in meeting him. I eagerly accepted his invitation. That I love Elton John certainly didn't hinder my acceptance!

I lived in Houston at the time, working as a paralegal for a friend who owned a law firm. My previous job in retail management in Chicago had relocated me to Houston to help open a new high-end furniture store near the Galleria. That job ended abruptly one afternoon when the general manager took me into her office and tearfully told me that she had to let me go. She said, "Shawn, sweetheart, I realize that you might not understand this right now, but I honestly feel like I'm doing you a favor. I do sincerely believe there is a big calling on your life of some sort and it's *not* in retail. I think you know that, too."

"I do", I anxiously replied. "But what am I going to do for now?"

"I'm not sure," she responded, "but I know you'll figure it out."

It was the second job from which I'd been fired in my life. The first one had been a retail position as well. I hated retail, and now the message was clear: I didn't belong there.

Throughout the two-hour flight from Houston to Los Angeles, I replayed the many conversations Cole and I had had. "Could he really be the sole heir of a Texas oil fortune?" I wondered. According to Cole, he was only a few years away from access to a trust that had been set up for him by his wealthy elderly mother. Not wanting her son to feel entitled by simply giving him everything, she'd required him to first forge his own path. Since she was a Christian, Cole was convinced that his coming out to his mother was also a contributing factor as to why she was afraid of being "too soft" on him. Even so, he said that he had done quite well for himself, establishing a successful interior-design business in Dallas and Los Angeles. Part of me wondered if his only interest in me was to appease his religious mother with an *ex-minister* boyfriend. Only time would tell. Circumstantially, because he was between homes in L.A., Cole said he would be putting us up at the Mondrian Hotel. Perfectly located on the Sunset Strip, the Mondrian was one of the favored temporary residences of several Hollywood A-listers during the Oscar weekend. He asked me if I would feel more comfortable with my own room or if we could share a suite. Since we had never met before, I took the safe way out and requested my own room.

The intense California sun danced off the polished chrome that perfectly outlined the black stretch limo that Cole had arranged to pick me up at LAX. As the chauffeur slowly pulled into the circular drive in front of the Mondrian, my sense of relief and heightened nervousness suddenly played tug-of-war with my emotions. "So far, so good," I thought, as the husky driver retrieved my suitcase from the trunk of the car. As I anxiously entered the hotel, the contemporary all-white lobby buzzed with activity. Soon, a tall, lanky bellboy led me into the elevator and up to the floor where my horseback-riding Texan awaited.

During the elevator ride, fragmented thoughts attempted to slow down my racing mind from the escalating apprehension I was feeling:

"Surely Cole is familiar with my attraction grid; the fitness trainer/underwear model I'd previously dated who had first given him my picture was a strikingly handsome guy."

"Cole sounded masculine and handsome over the phone, didn't he?"

The elevator stopped. The bellboy escorted me to the hotel-room door. The door opened. My heart sank. Cole was not my type, not at all.

With his red hair spiked and overly gelled, his freckled face, and his head-to-toe haute couture ensemble, Cole presented very little that read as masculine, other than possibly his tanned, leathery complexion. From the moment he opened his mouth, his purse fell out. He stood with one hip cocked to the side as he held a Louis Vuitton bag stuffed with a fluffy white poodle, fetchingly strapped to his shoulder, only adding to my distress at how different he looked than he had sounded on the phone.

I tried my best to hide my disappointment, quickly readjusting what must have been an expression of utter shock. It wasn't easy. Walking towards me with evident intention, he leaned forward for a kiss. With a quick head turn to the right, I blocked it, grabbing him for a hug. It couldn't have been more awkward. To make matters worse, he informed me that he was waiting to hear back from the front desk regarding their efforts to fix their mistake and find us a second room.

With the Oscar weekend in full swing, the best they could do was to put us both in a larger suite. We were soon ushered in to what appeared to be a fully accommodating space until I soon discovered that there was only one king-sized bed. Cole told me not to worry; he would gladly sleep on the sofa.

I wasn't buying any of it.

From that moment on, Cole proceeded to put forth a parade of efforts to wine, dine, and dazzle me into permanent-boyfriend status. It started with his encouraging me try on a flamboyant $16,000 dinner jacket that his mother had commissioned a famous designer to stitch for him, as well as gold-and- diamond cufflinks that Cole claimed had been given to his father by the Shah of Iran. That night after we finished dinner at a Beverly Hills hot spot, we made our way to a hip new bar to meet up with a few of his friends for music and drinks. I must have spent an hour or so talking to Cole's friend Edwin, the young son of the famed photographer known for his many iconic photographs of Marilyn Monroe. After we relaxed over a few Cape Cods and he'd learned of my pastoral background, he began to open up to me about the challenges of finding genuine friends in L.A. He said, "Everyone is so fake here, always looking over their shoulder to make their next connection. I honestly find it difficult at times to read whether people really like me for me or if they're just using me."

In the midst of a crowd of perfect faces, I found the sincerity of Edwin's raw, authentic expression the most attractive of all. He appeared to be a genuinely nice guy, someone I would enjoy hanging out with if I lived there. Before we left, he commented to me, "You're nothing like the guys that Cole has previously dated; I hope you stick around." Having learned earlier in the day that Cole's ex-boyfriend, a professional tennis player, was quite the diva, I took this as a compliment.

After we returned to the hotel, I said to Cole that he could sleep in the king-size bed with me as long as he promised to stay on his own side. However, when morning came, I woke up facing the wall, hanging slightly off the edge of that California king with Cole spooning me from behind and breathing heavily on the back of my neck. I quickly and quietly slipped out of the bed and retreated to the bathroom for a long, hot shower behind a locked door. Unfortunately for Cole, my alcohol goggles were not *that* cloudy.

Waiting in front of the hotel for the car to pick us up for dinner that evening, I was agog when I spotted a big Hollywood star I'd grown up watching in the movies standing only a few feet away. I smiled as she looked in my direction, and surprisingly, she returned the gesture. However, within seconds, I lost my nerve and quickly looked away. In some peculiar way, simply holding the snapshot of her smile in my mind, made me feel just a little bit taller in the intimidating surroundings where I felt so out of place. It also provided me a boost of confidence as Cole and I headed to a popular restaurant to dine with his actor friend along with the actor's new Canadian girlfriend, who was currently playing a character in the most popular show on TV. After arriving at the luxurious eatery, Cole's connections became evident when the waiter walked us to one of the premier tables, nestled at the front of the towering balcony, presenting a clear view of everyone below. When we were seated, the general manager came to the table to greet us with a bottle of Champagne and to briefly sit down for a visit with Cole. It was a lot to take in. Having been seated next to the blonde, blue-eyed Canadian woman, I didn't take long to hit it off with her. Within minutes, we were laughing and chatting like old friends. By the time we were finished eating, she was adamant that I needed to move to L.A. and try my hand at the entertainment business. She said if I were up to it, she would personally help me secure an audition for a soap opera. She was such a sweetheart, so animated and unpretentious. Her good-looking, narcissistic boyfriend? Let's just say it was easy to see why he and Cole were such good friends.

Throughout the evening, I cringed every time Cole put his hand on my leg under the table. When he eventually tried to hold my hand, I quickly grabbed my napkin off my lap and wiped my mouth. As I focused on the bubbles floating to the top of my fresh glass of Champagne poured by the waiter, I could feel my anger instantly rising. *"Why doesn't he get it?!"* I shouted in my head, *"I'm NOT into him!"* But as I retreated to the restroom for a brief period to clear my head, I could begin to see there was more going on under the surface.

I had zero attraction to Cole, but deep down, gnawing at my emotions was a fearful part of me that *wanted* to be.

When I walked away from the ministry, I felt as though I'd also walked away from a profound sense of purpose. For years I'd lived content that I was somehow a valuable part of changing people's lives. Dealing with an out-of-control customer about a miniscule scratch on her dining room table wasn't enough for me. Working as a paralegal wasn't enough for me. I felt lost.

All the career assessments I'd taken after my separation from Andrea pointed me back to the kind of work I'd done in the ministry. I knew that the calling on my life as a creative communicator was evident, but how to get back into it as a gay man felt like an unreachable task. My entire network and contacts were all in the Christian arena and I had been warned by the vice-president of the large organization where I'd previously worked that he would stop me if he heard of my speaking or singing again. Adding to the distress of my circumstances were my bachelor's degree in theology and all of my work experience embedded in various church-ministry positions. How would I support myself? What would I do with the rest of my life?

My old-familiar feelings of inadequacy and incompetence increased, following me like an incorrigible horsefly. I'd spent all of my adult life ensconced inside a Christian bubble and was quite unprepared for this frightening new world in which I existed. I was tired—tired of the drama, tired of being taken advantage of, and tired of living aimlessly.

Walking on the beach earlier that afternoon, Cole had tempted me with a way out.

"Shawn, there is no reason why you can't get back into ministry and music," he gently offered. "Let me help you. I actually have an idea that could help us both. I've often thought how I would love to put together a large LGBT Christian conference on our family ranch in Montana. I just didn't know how to go about making it happen. You do!" he added with growing excitement. "That's right in your wheelhouse. I could be the financial backer and you could be one of the speakers and organize the whole thing."

I couldn't believe what I was hearing, but his seemingly generous offer didn't stop there.

"I can't imagine how difficult all this change has been for you. Why don't you think about letting me put you on my business payroll? You can live here in my LA residence and focus completely on your music. I'm friends with a very talented music producer here in LA whom I would love to introduce you to while you're here. I called her and she said she could join us for church on Sunday morning and talk with you after the service if you're up for it."

"Thank you; I would love to," I said, trying to appear calm and mask my enthusiasm.

But the thrill didn't last for long, because I knew that there would be many strings attached, and those strings would eventually become chains. The question that kept turning in my head was, *"Could I at least do it for a limited period of time?"*

After dinner, we went back to the big house in the Hollywood Hills that Cole's friend shared with a movie producer. We hung out in the game room and drank by the pool until the sun came up. I had too much on my mind. I couldn't have slept anyway.

Cole kept his promise. On Oscar Sunday, I met the music producer he had told me about. She shared with me that she was currently working with a major athlete/reality-TV star. A beautiful, well-spoken black woman, she reminded me of one my close friends in high school who often accompanied me on the piano. She had been my date to junior prom. Meeting this producer was a definite pluck on my heart strings, especially after being brought to tears by the moving contemporary worship music we'd just heard in the church service.

On the ride back to the hotel, I hardly spoke a word. The conversation I was having in my head left little room for anything else. After Cole and I quickly freshened up in our room before going down to the hotel restaurant for lunch, persistent Cole made yet another attempt to kiss me, which I once again diverted with a hug.

With obvious frustration, after we ordered our lunch at our table by the window, Cole turned to me and said, "Shawn, I just don't get it! Do you have any idea what I'm offering you? You have pushed me away the entire time you've been here. Why would you just throw this opportunity away? I have the capability of making all your dreams come true; don't you know that?"

Anger has always shut me down, and I went completely numb as I stared blankly at the floor.

After several minutes, Cole snatched up his phone and walked away from the table. When he returned, I looked at him and sincerely said, "Cole, I really appreciate your flying me out here, but I have to be honest with you: I just don't have feelings like that for you."

Dismissively, he said, "Well, I was able to snag just one seat at the Oscars tonight, so you'll be on your own. Your flight leaves tomorrow at noon."

I put my hand on his and said as sweetly as I could, "Cole, I'm really sorry; I am." As we both sat there looking disillusioned, I softly asked, "Is it possible for me to fly home today?"

Just hours before the Elton John party I had so looked forward to, I returned home to my modest Houston apartment and my unfulfilling job at the law office.

CHAPTER 10

———— ♋ ————

ALMOST A YEAR later, I met Matt at a three-day circuit party in Austin and we instantly fell for each other. I'd never been so taken by someone. He was a triathlete with a great body—cute, successful, and incredibly thoughtful. Discovering that we both shared strong ties to Christianity and had similar struggles with our sexuality made us especially attracted to each other.

Three weeks after our first encounter, Matt said that our daily phone conversations were no longer enough for him, so he flew me out to his home in San Diego for a visit. He had arranged a small house party, inviting some of his closest friends to meet me when I arrived. After an hour or so, we couldn't wait for them to leave; we both had only one thing on our minds.

Previously an actor in New York and Hollywood, Matt had returned to college in his thirties and finished his undergraduate degree in genetics, and then earned his MBA. His return to college paralleled his return to the closet, and he also joined Exodus International (the Christian based anti-gay reparative therapy group) and a twelve-step program to deal with his alcoholism.

He eventually moved to San Diego, re-emerged from the closet, and landed a position as vice president of a medical-device startup company just a couple years before we met. He wasn't wealthy by California standards, but was definitely in a far better financial place than I was.

Every three weeks for four months, I flew to San Diego or Matt flew to Houston. During our visits in either city, he paid for everything. I'd never before felt so taken care of as I did when I was with him. He seemed to possess an uncommon awareness of seeing people's needs before they expressed them and doing what he could to help; I was so impressed by that. In San Diego, Matt worked as a volunteer, delivering meals to shut-ins with AIDS. There were so many things about him that tugged at my pastoral heart and made me fall deeper for him. He often complemented me and was very intuitive and observant concerning my secret struggles with my body and sex. Matt helped me become more comfortable with myself. I was so grateful for his sensitivity to my insecurities. Greater confidence was something I desperately needed, and he was giving me that.

Toward the end of those four months, Matt asked me to move out to San Diego and live with him. He assured me that if I did, he would take care of everything. I knew in my heart it was way too soon, but he had a way of calming my fears by addressing all my concerns with a well thought-out plan.

I had no savings to bring to the relationship; only some nice furniture and home accessories that I'd acquired while working at the high-end furniture store. Matt said he loved my style, and one of the ways I could contribute was by using my decorating abilities to set up a home for us. He also emphasized that I wouldn't have to worry about finding a high-paying job, but could focus on something that I would enjoy, such as a position with a non-profit organization. Matt was adamant about our sharing everything, "just like a married couple." He said that would put me on his bank accounts and credit cards so that I would feel secure. Matt was very persuasive when he wanted something, and he made it extremely difficult for me to say no.

It appeared as though I'd finally met my prince, and he was about to whisk me away to live with him in one of the most beautiful places in the country.

My best friend Ryan had arranged a dinner party with a few of our friends in Houston one weekend when Matt was in town. They had already decided that they loved Matt, but wanted a more intimate opportunity to get to know him better. As the evening progressed and we all had several glasses of wine, I excused myself from the table to visit the restroom. A few minutes after I returned, I noticed that Matt was responding to me a little differently, but I blamed it on the wine. After dinner finished and my friends were busy entertaining each other, I took Matt on a quick tour of Ryan's lovely townhouse. On the way back down from the top floor, he blocked me on the stairs.

With an accusatory tone, Matt asked, "Why was Stan looking at you like that?" My mind began to race. I had absolutely no idea what he was talking about. I smiled nervously, assuring him that it was nothing, but he wouldn't let it go. Moving in closer and grabbing my wrist, he said. "I saw the way he was looking you up and down when you came out of the bathroom, and I saw you smile back at him!"

I was completely blindsided. I felt like I had when my stepfather Jed used to accuse me of doing something unimaginable to my little sister. I blanked out and didn't know how to respond. I shut down.

For several minutes I sat on the stairs, looking at the wall as Matt continued to intimidate me with his uninterrupted stare. A voice deep inside of me screamed, *"SHAWN, THIS IS A BAD SIGN!"*

Suddenly, his demeanor completely changed; he smiled and said, "It's okay, sweetheart. Let's just forget about it."

I felt like someone had knocked me onto the floor, only to turn around and say, "You can get up now; I was just kidding!"

I felt confused and disappointed, but chose to not share with anyone what had happened at Ryan's, and tried my best to convince myself that the whole thing had been exacerbated by the wine. I remembered that Matt had previously told me that he struggled with jealousy and was working on it. So I rationalized, *"Isn't the most important part that he's working on it?"*

It didn't seem to faze me that this pivotal conversation was taking place completely in my head. I was unwilling and afraid to give anyone else the opportunity to talk me out of what I wanted to be real, even though there had been several other incidents akin to that incident on the stairs.

There was also a part of me that didn't want to look stupid for picking the wrong person again, and letting everyone else down.

Prior to moving to San Diego, I went to see gay-rights activist Mel White speak at a small church in Houston. Mel's autobiography, *Stranger at the Gate*, had had a powerful impact on me when I first left the ministry. Previously a ghostwriter for one of the most notable Christian evangelists of our time, Mel had joined the staff of Cathedral of Hope in Dallas, at the time the largest LGBT church in the world, after he came out.

While I was staying with my best friend, a traveling worship leader, in Tulsa for a few months after Andrea and I separated, I became friends with a gay Christian ER doctor who gave me Mel's book.

The doctor, who was still semi-closeted and a leader in his church, had come out to his pastor, his pastor's wife, and his best friend. His pastor was a well-loved TV evangelist and his best friend was the most famous contemporary Christian singer in the world. Although his pastor and his friend truly loved him, they struggled with his being gay. The pastor's wife, however, was completely behind him and his strongest advocate. She fully believed the credible research that substantiates people being born gay.

When I started reading Mel's book, I couldn't put it down. I related with so much of it: his years in ministry, the struggles of being married to a woman, and the deep cry in his heart to live authentically. The encouragement and strength I found in the pages of Mel's book, and from the conversations I had with my new gay Christian friend, proved to me that I was not alone and provided me the courage to keep moving forward.

After hearing Mel speak in Houston, now two years later, I met with him briefly afterward and shared some of my own story. Most of the time I saw people's eyes glaze over when I talked about God and my time in the ministry, but in Mel White's eyes, I saw only empathy. It had been a long time since I had felt genuinely understood. Mel said he was well familiar with the training institute where I had taught in Dallas, and he asked me what I wanted to do next.

"Ministry is in my heart," I said, "and I really see myself as a speaker, but I honestly don't even know where to start."

He kindly told me that he would love to help me any way that he could. When he learned that I was about to move to California with my boyfriend, he invited both of us to come up to San Francisco, where he and his partner had recently moved, and meet with them. I was so excited by his offer. I believed it to be the opportunity that I'd been praying for. After so much uncertainty, it seemed as though things were finally beginning to fall in line for me.

When I told Matt about this opportunity, all he could say was, "Shawn, that guy just wants to get in your pants. Trust me, I know all about those kinds of gay guys."

I had not felt that vibe from Mel at all, but just as I had with the Nashville producer years before when I was married to Andrea, I stuffed my disappointment way down inside of myself, and sadly let the opportunity slip away.

The view from Matt's and my living room in the Mission Hills area of San Diego afforded a stunning view of downtown, the ocean, and a section of the sprawling two-mile bridge to Coronado Island. The coolest part was our distant view of commercial airplanes landing at the downtown airport—the only one of its kind in the middle of a major US city. From our house perched on a hill, it appeared as though these giant metal birds were flying directly into the towering skyscrapers.

Matt had rented a 1980s-style modern house for us. It was rather outdated, but the fireplace, large deck with a Jacuzzi, location, and views, all made it well worth its price. Soon after I moved in, Matt wanted to have a housewarming party and invite all his friends. The timing wouldn't give us very long do all the work, but we agreed that it could be fun to take on the challenge, so we did.

The day the truck arrived from Houston with all my furniture and home décor, I worked tirelessly without eating, unpacking and arranging as much as I could before Matt got home. I wanted to surprise him. I was in the master bedroom putting some things away when he finally came home from the office that evening.

He walked in, put his things down, and said nothing.

The entire time we were eating dinner, Matt acted coldly toward me. I started feeling uncomfortable. I tried to lighten up his mood by filling him in on the comical challenges the movers had in getting the furniture up the steep hill to our house. Without responding to my story, he angrily snapped at me, saying, "Why are you trying to control everything?"

Completely confused by his question, I responded, "What do you mean?"

"You know what I mean!" he said hatefully, "I can't believe you would do all this decorating without me!"

My feathers fell. "I'm sorry you're so upset," I quickly replied. "You are so confusing to me!" I said, burying my face in my hands.

My survival instincts kicked in, and I stood up for myself. "Matt, you told me on several occasions that you wanted me to decorate our home. I was just following through with what you said YOU wanted! How is that being controlling? I actually wanted to surprise you today!

It's not that big a deal. We can change things around if you don't like where they are. Why are you so angry?!"

Raising his voice, he responded, "I was at the office all day working hard, and I come home to see how much fun you were having decorating. I wish I could stay home all day, just decorating!"

The disillusionment I felt began to push out the tears as we sat in silence. He eventually shoved his chair back from the dining table and stomped off. I went out onto the balcony, closed the glass door behind myself, and cried.

A few weeks later, Matt and I joined several of his friends at a huge outdoor party during the Super Bowl, which was in San Diego that year. Matt told me that his friends had been complaining to him that they hadn't had the opportunity to spend enough time getting to know me. He was excited that we would have the entire night to hang out with them.

About an hour after we arrived, Matt strangely said that he wasn't feeling like being out and he was going to go back home. I said, "Okay, I'll go with you." "No, you stay here," he said adamantly. "I'll be fine. I want you to have fun with my friends," he said with a sincere tone. "They'll take care of you."

"Are you sure, Matt?" I hesitantly replied.

Grabbing both of my hands, while facing me and looking into my eyes, he said "Yes, Shawn, I'm positive. "Stay and have fun!"

I felt like the whole thing seemed a little odd, but went along with it. I blew it off as Matt's possibly wanting some alone time to recharge, which I could certainly understand.

An hour and a half after Matt left, while we were all standing around listening to one of the bands perform, Matt called his friend Anthony's cell phone to check on me. I had left my phone at home, so I playfully grabbed Anthony's phone to see how Matt was doing. "Hi, Matt! Are you doing okay?" I asked lovingly.

"How do you think I'm doing?!" he responded with obvious anger. The sudden fear I felt quickly squelched all the fun I'd been having, as I turned away from Matt's friends and said, "Matt, what's wrong?"

"You know what's wrong!" he responded hatefully. "I can't believe that you would stay there without me!"

I was completely dumbfounded. In Matt's twisted mind the whole thing was obviously a set up from the beginning. Once again, he was testing me to see if I would live up to his hidden expectations.

The rest of the night was hell.

Matt's unpredictable behavior quickly unraveled my fragile emotions. He was full of contradictions and often seemed to have a hidden agenda. His abrupt style of cross-examining me out of the blue, even though I generally had no idea what he was talking about, started to make me question myself.

It became apparent that Matt was both jealous of others *wanting* me, and also strangely jealous *of* me. He was a decade older and very competitive. When guys paid attention to me and approached me, he would give me the cold shoulder as though I'd had something to do with it. If the tables were turned and the attention was on him, he was happy and in a great mood. Over time, I found myself instantly looking at the floor when we entered the gym just to avoid his constantly asking me who I was looking at.

His scrutiny was exhausting!

When things were good between Matt and me, they were really good—some of the best times I'd had up until that period of my life. But when things were bad, they were awful. I felt like I was living with two completely different people, and I never knew which one was going to show up at any given time.

This back-and-forth dynamic made our life so confusing for me. I'd learned to survive the dark places of life by focusing on the good in front of me and using it as a lighthouse to guide me forward. Being in a relationship of such extremes made things almost impossible for me to process.

I felt like I was the helpless child all over again, trapped in a new psychological thriller with my mean stepfather.

Loneliness was cruel to me in San Diego. I missed my friends back in Houston terribly. The angry guy I worked with four days a week overseeing a Catholic family homeless shelter was a bitter old queen who frightened me. The only other people I knew were Matt's friends. I didn't feel like I had anyone I could trust or open up to.

Nicholas, a successful lawyer from a famous Texas political family, and his life-partner Tommy, who owned a landscape-architecture business, were two of my closet friends in Houston, and I'd stayed in contact with them. Over the months they had become quite concerned about me after several emotionally charged phone calls.

Late one morning after yet another dramatic night with Matt, I called Nicholas at his office. By the time we ended the call, he had convinced me to allow Tommy to fly out to San Diego and move me back to Houston. Nicholas said he would pay for everything and that I could stay with them as long as I needed until I got back on my feet. When I ended my conversation with Nicholas, I was bombarded with a profusion of emotions like tiny pieces of shrapnel invading my heart. I sat in silence for what seemed like hours until eventually, the stinging sensation on my face brought by dried salty tears demanded my attention.

I was done.

When Tommy arrived In San Diego a few days later to help me load up my things, it was so difficult for me to go. Since I'd told him I was leaving, Matt had completely turned up his charismatic charm and ultra-caring composure to the highest mode possible. It melted me every time.

Even though Matt had hurt me deeply, I cried for several hours after Tommy and I loaded up the trailer hitched to my car and started out on our long trip back to Houston. I really did love Matt, and I was so disappointed, wishing things could have been different.

It was New Year's Eve when Tommy and I stopped for the night in Phoenix. After we checked into a hotel and got cleaned up, he wanted to take me out dinner and dancing to cheer me up a bit. Following a good meal and a few drinks at the hotel restaurant, we called a cab to take us to a gay dance club. The cab never showed.

The desert weather was refreshingly cool but not cold that evening, so we decided to make an adventure of it and walk. Tommy, with his witty sense of humor, knew how to make me laugh, but our laughter that evening was short lived as we embarked on a shady part of town that made us both feel nervous. As we picked up our pace, chatting about our misconception on the distance from the hotel to the club, we suddenly heard steps behind us.

Slowing down only long enough to momentarily exchange mutual glances of concern was all it took. We were both instantly stopped dead in our tracks by the shimmer of a knife blade in our faces. "I cut you! I cut you!" said the large Hispanic guy, dressed in black, with a buzzed haircut and a thick accent. The angry look on his face indicated that he meant business and his physical size supported his intention. "Money! Give me! Money!" he demanded, firmly shaking the knife.

"Okay, okay!" Tommy said, putting up one hand to try to calm our attacker and the other in his pocket. As Tommy handed him all his cash, his face completely white from fear, the tattooed one turned his attention to me waving his knife.

"You! Money!"

Before I had time to reason, I threw up both hands shaking my head saying, "No money, no money!"

I did have some cash and a credit card in my front pocket, but my survival instinct won out over my fear, since it was all the money I had to my name. Our dimwitted mugger let us go. Shaking his knife in our faces one last time, he shouted, "Run! Run! You die if you look!"

We believed him, running like marathoners until we located a police officer to report the incident. We were shaken up and very winded, but safe. Unfortunately, Tommy lost $2,000 and his watch that night.

We didn't do any dancing that night.

Depression, fear, and increased anxiety bounced me around like a ping-pong ball after I returned to Houston. Every time I ran into someone who had attended my going-away party that Nicholas and Tommy had hosted for me prior to my moving to San Diego, I wanted to hide. I felt like a fool again. The one who had been the envy of all his friends for finding passionate love and pursing it with reckless abandon had skulked back into town, heartbroken and jobless.

When Matt started calling me again a few weeks later with a new plan, I once again naively opened my heart to him. He said that he had found a therapist who would work with us, and he would be willing to do whatever it took to get me back. He promised me things would be different. I believed him.

Nicholas and Tommy were furious at me, but I returned to San Diego. The senior male therapist Matt had hired for us? Our unconventional private sessions, with him sitting between my legs, facing me, while he tapped on my knees, absolutely repulsed me. They called to mind the time Brother Duff, a visiting minister from Scotland, laid his hands on my genitals to pray for me in an isolated pew when I told him I was struggling with impure thoughts and masturbation. I was a young, gullible minister at the time, in my early twenties, and was so enthralled by this highly respected man of faith that I completely spiritualized the incident and kept it to myself. The intense shame I felt afterward, I believed, was God allowing me to feel the depth of my sin. Now, this therapist seated between my legs wanted me to focus on certain events in my past, and all I wanted to do was run from him.

The therapy sessions Matt and I had together were incredibly uncomfortable for me as well. I never felt that I could be completely honest.

When Matt let it out one night while we were drinking that he was occasionally talking to the therapist about me over the phone, I shut down even more.

Nothing changed, and Matt's unpredictable behavior and jealousy only escalated.

As I stood on the towering cliff overlooking the ocean, reliving all that had happened, I wanted to jump. I was in so much pain, so tired of the endless mind games. My dark, self-deprecating thoughts slowly pushed me toward the edge.

"Why didn't you stay in Houston when your friend flew out here to rescue you the first time? Shawn, you're so stupid for burning that bridge! Now you have no way out!"

"You're such a failure! You have no personal money, and your part-time job at the Children's Treatment Center is not enough to support you. You idiot, you're completely stuck!"

"How could you allow him to sweet talk you back into this nightmare?! You've judged your mother for going back to that madman Jed again and again. You are just like her!"

In my darkness, I concluded that I had only one option.

CHAPTER 11

—— ✥ ——

THE MASSIVE OLD magnolia trees draped in Spanish moss and the sprawl-ing, columned front porches repeated a reminder: I wasn't on the West Coast any more.

As I drove deeper into Mississippi, I failed to realize the depth of my anxiety until both of my hands fell numb from their prolonged grip on the steering wheel. I momentarily snapped out of the trance I'd been in for what seemed like hours, obsessing over my fate. I was terrified.

I felt as though I were about to turn myself over to the governing au-thorities to do with me as they chose. Realistically, I knew had no con-trol over what that would be. It felt drastically different from the sense of freedom and liberation I'd felt on the streets of Chicago shortly after coming out a few years earlier.

Somewhere along my lonely trek across the country from California, shame, humiliation, and judgment had jumped into the back seat of my car and they hounded me for the rest of the trip. The depression I'd fallen into while in San Diego seemed to darken with each mile as I drove closer to the door which would inevitably lead me back into the dreaded closet.

As I slowly pulled into Gulfport, I recalled the times Andrea and I had min-istered there. We'd traveled there once on tour with our worship band

and another time to speak at a weekend seminar. The congregation and its kindhearted pastor, Robert Bianchi, had become very dear to us. We became friends and he eventually offered us positions on his church staff. Although Andrea and I were sincerely touched by his invitation, we had no interest in moving from Dallas to a small town in Mississippi.

Robert had called me a few times to check on me after I left Andrea. His voice messages carried a much kinder and more loving tone than most of the others I received. He seemed to be more concerned about me than about just my ministry. I never forgot that.

When I reached out to Robert by phone on that dire day as I stood on the cliff in San Diego, he didn't hesitate for a moment to ask me to come and stay with him and his family. His unexpected exposure to my twisted emotions and endless questions that afternoon would have tested the patience and empathy of any seasoned minister, but he remained compassionate and supportive. I'm sure he realized that bringing me into his home with his family could be messy, but even so, he assured me by saying, "Shawn, we love you and we want you to be safe. Just get here, my friend, and we'll figure it out together with God's help."

Safe: That's all he had to say. The quest for safety had driven me down the street to the little white church when I was seven years old, and now it would drive me all the way from California to Mississippi in my thirties.

It was among the churched that I experienced and knew God to be, and a deep part of me desperately needed to feel close to God again.

Robert was kind, mild-tempered, small in stature, with the heart of a giant. A brilliant man with a master's in divinity from Princeton, he possessed a rare humility which was luring and infectious.

Viola, Robert's nurturing wife, had a dramatic persona (reminiscent of Fran Drescher's character on the television sitcom "The Nanny"), with curly black hair and a thick New Orleans accent; she was the mother of their two endearing children, Lauren and Christopher.

Just prior to my arrival, Lauren had graduated from college and married her fiancé Joshua, also a pastor's kid. They made a strikingly beautiful couple, inside and out. They were staying with Lauren's parents for the summer until they moved to Nashville for Lauren to begin graduate school in the fall. Christopher, Lauren's younger brother, was the athlete in the family and on a fast track to finishing high school.

When all the Bianchis were together, they sounded like the stereotypical Italian family, laughing and excitedly talking over each other. What I didn't see coming was how deeply I'd fall in love with this family, and in such a short time.

The way Robert exemplified Jesus by serving his family was unlike anything I'd seen from any other man. I never tired of witnessing the skillful way he often used his art for cooking in such an extraordinary way to be present for his family. At various times throughout the week, I would see Robert humming away in the kitchen while cooking something for his wife or one of his children. After he served them with great love and care, he would pull up a chair next to them in the breakfast nook to do his best work of all: to listen and encourage.

Robert often extended this same invitation to me. His selfless gesture never failed to warm my heart, but due to the messy heap of emotional garbage I carried, I never felt comfortable or worthy of it. I felt completely demoralized and humiliated staying with the Bianchis. I had devolved into a broken shell of the capable minister they had once admired.

139

It was evident, though, that the way I felt inside had nothing to do with them. They treated me with the utmost love and respect from the beginning, and often went overboard to make me feel a part of their family.

Shortly before moving to San Diego, I had been broadsided while driving in Houston, reinjuring my back and neck. As a result, I'd been seeing a chiropractor the entire time I lived with Matt. The three-day car trip to Mississippi, along with leaving my gym membership back in San Diego (along with all of my furniture), worsened my back pain. Because I was unable to sleep on the floor, Christopher gave up his room for me during the summer months while Lauren and Joshua were staying with the Bianchis. I never once heard this teenager complain or make any sign of annoyance for agreeing to sleep on a blow-up mattress out on the screened porch. His maturity and selflessness at such a young age amazed me.

Robert soon informed me that he was taking me to see an orthopedic specialist who was a member of their church congregation, to see if there was something he could do to help me.

I felt anxious about the appointment because I remembered that Andrea and I had had dinner with this same young doctor and his wife years before.

My anxiety proved to be warranted. The warm, friendly person I remembered had been replaced by a cold, stoic character who barely looked at me during the entire examination process. I couldn't help thinking that his behavior communicated to me, "You're getting exactly what you deserve!" I wanted to disappear.

I knew Robert was only trying to help me, so I shared little of my experience with him. I never went back to see that doctor again.

During my six-month stay with the Bianchis, hanging out with Lauren and Joshua proved to be some of the best times I'd had in ages. The shame I struggled with at first around them must've been very noticeable at times, because Joshua came right out and told me he felt "zero weirdness" around me. He assured me that he and Lauren felt nothing but admiration for me. Their actions caused me to believe them.

It was unusual that the three of us connected so quickly and I felt so comfortable around them. We went to movies, hung out at Barnes & Noble drinking coffee, and sometimes just sat around laughing and talking about life.

Joshua was working part time as a worship leader at a local church and was constantly picking my brain about music ministry. His eagerness to learn and his teachable heart provided me a temporary but greatly needed sense of purpose. I pulled out some of the old video footage I had from the days Andrea and I traveled with the worship band and used it as a point of reference to teach him some things I'd learned along the way.

I was surprised at how watching those old videos helped me reconnect with a part of myself that felt so far removed. Through the recorded footage of those powerful moments, I could still feel the tangible presence of God.

One of the first challenging items on my list after arriving at the Bianchis was to call my family back in Ohio and come clean with them about my post-ministry activities. I'd never told them all that had happened after I left Andrea; only the parts I thought they wanted to hear. When I moved out to San Diego with Matt, I lied to them, saying I was living with an old ministry buddy I knew from my time pastoring in

California. Although I'd spoken with them somewhat regularly, I'd kept them completely in the dark about my sexuality.

My relationship with my family had changed drastically over the years after I recommitted my life to God and made the decision to go into full-time ministry. The shift began with a simple phone call I made to Mom and Jed one evening while I was away at school in my freshmen year of college:

"Hi, Mom," I said tenderly. "Sorry it's been a while since you've heard from me. I've been really busy with my classes."

"It's okay, honey," she said. "It's good to hear from you!"

"Actually, I...I don't have a lot to say," I continued with a deliberate tone, "but I wanted to see if I could talk with you and Jed both for a minute."

Clearly surprised and with a hint of concern, she said, "Oh, o-kay?! Let me see if he's awake from his nap, and if I can get him to pick up the other phone."

As I waited for Jed to join our conversation, my heart palpitated. I closed my eyes tightly as I prayed for strength.

"Hey, Bud! How's it goin'?" Jed mumbled.

"It's going good; thanks for getting on the phone," I nervously responded. "I just wanted to s-a-ay something to you and Mom together."

"Okay, cool," he said, "What is it?"

Everything in me wanted to play it safe, but I took off running to the edge of the ravine, grabbed hold of a vine of courage, and jumped.

"I just wanted to tell you both that I forgive you," I said. "I forgive you for the abuse, and I forgive you for all the pain you put me through." After what seemed like several minutes of silence, I added, "I just wanted you both to know that. I love you and I'll talk to you later." With that, I hung up. It was done.

Up until that time, just the memory of Jed's face or speaking his name in conversation would twist my gut into knots, but what I did that evening when I was eighteen years old brought me a life-altering spiritual experience. All the hate and bitterness I'd carried for so long washed away, and the tide carried with it my serial nightmares of Jed killing us all, which I'd endured since childhood.

My fear had lifted.

Not long after that phone call, I moved back home for a short period of time before I transferred to a Christian college in southern Illinois to study contemporary Christian music. Several people in my life were greatly disappointed about my decision to go into ministry instead of pursuing a career in musical theater. My friend Corinne came right out and bluntly told me that I was throwing my life away. My mom, who had finally separated from and was divorcing Jed, also expressed unhappiness about my decision.

I tried my best to help my mom out while I was home by changing the tires on her new Jeep multiple times because Jed continued to slice them in the night, and repainting the interior of her house, which she had recently purchased after years of renting. However, our lifestyles couldn't have been more contrasting at that point. I continuously studied my Bible, spent time with my church friends, and grew more self-righteous by the day, while Mom went out every night drinking with her girlfriends.

I went downstairs one morning to see a guy with whom I'd gone to high school on our sofa, passed out from partying with my mom the night before. I decided to go stay with a friend's family until I left again for school.

Greatly concerned that Mom was quickly spinning out of control, I eventually went to see her supervisor at work and begged her to force her into treatment. She told me that my mother was still showing up to work every day on time, and that she was sorry, but there was nothing she could do.

The next year while I was studying at my new college in Illinois, I received a phone call from my grandmother informing me that Mom had been charged with a felony for stealing money from the company that employed her. Jed had talked her into fleeing with him to New Orleans to stay with his brother and avoid being arrested. My greatest fear for her had come true: She'd lost everything! My car that Mom had been helping me pay for was repossessed, but somehow, I managed to stay in college.

Fortunately, Grandma was not living with Mom any longer at the time Mom fled to Louisiana with Jed. Grandma had been left a little money from her ex-husband Roy when he suddenly died of a stroke. She used the windfall to move into a high-rise for seniors, where two of her relatives also lived.

Grandma's one-bedroom apartment was small, but she'd purchased new furniture and had it decorated just as she liked it. I slept on her sofa bed in the living room a few times when I went back to Ohio during my Christmas break from school. Obviously, living there on her own, free from the toxic environment she'd been circumstantially forced into for so many years with Mom and Jed, was just what she needed. Grandma was back to her old loving and creative self, happier than I'd seen her in years. Overjoyed that her beloved grandson was now preparing for the ministry, she eagerly reconnected with me.

During one of my visits, I was able to begin opening up to Grandma about some of the pain of my childhood. The big difference between Grandma and Mom was that Grandma was willing to go there with me. Mom never was.

The hardest conversation I had with Grandma at that time involved her own son, my mom's youngest brother Noah.

When I was four years old, Mom and I stayed with Grandma and Grandpa Roy for a while after Mom left Dad. One evening while the house was full of guests and everyone was sitting around the table enjoying conversation and laughter, my seventeen-year-old Uncle Noah molested me in his bedroom.

Noah was my favorite uncle because he was always fun and often played with me. When I went searching for him that evening to see what he was up to, I discovered him sitting on his bed naked, with only a sheet barely covering his groin. He didn't physically hurt me, but what happened that night in his bedroom mentally and emotionally vexed me for years.

When it was over, I knew something was wrong because I felt dirty. The fact he had me laughing from the start and made the whole thing like a game was incredibly confusing to my little mind and body.

After I left Noah's bedroom, I went into the kitchen and stood beside Grandma's chair as she sat around the table with the others. Eventually, I put my arm around her and leaned into her ear, whispering to her what had just happened in Noah's room.

Grandma quickly jumped up from the table and snatched me up by the arm. She then marched me to the guest room where she angrily spanked me, insisting I never talk like that again. In a way that she had never talked to me before, Grandma said, "Now you just stay in here for a while!" She shut the door and left me alone in the dark as I climbed up on the bed and cried myself to sleep.

Although Uncle Noah never did anything like that again, the incident, along with my grandmother's response, did some deep damage to my developing mind. If my sweet grandmother, whom I loved dearly, wouldn't protect me when someone hurt me, and even punished me for talking about it, I must have deserved it. It only added to my growing belief that I was worthless.

As I sat on the footstool in front of Grandma's chair at the age of twenty, taking a chance to reopen this painful moment that had been locked away and unresolved for so long, her response was completely different. A look of agony fell on her face as her eyes filled with tears. Although she said she didn't remember the incident, she wasted no time taking both of my hands, saying, "Shawn, I'm so sorry, sweetheart! I'm sorry Noah did that to you! I'm sorry I hurt you like that! Please forgive me!

Finally, the healing came, as we hugged and cried together that afternoon.

As I reflected later that evening on the emotional event I'd had with my grandmother, I realized it hadn't been her words of forgiveness I'd longed for the most; it was her simple acknowledgment of my pain and suffering that I had craved.

I was working about an hour outside of St. Louis in my first ministry position when my mom decided to return to Ohio and face her demons. I had so much respect for the courage required of her to do the right thing. After she served her jail sentence, she began dealing with her alcoholism, started attending a local church, and slowly began to rebuild her life. Struggling to take care of my sister on her own with a felony on her record, Mom eventually asked Grandma to leave her apartment in the retirement high-rise and rent a place with her. The decision wasn't easy for Grandma. She really loved where she was living and the new friends she'd made, but she couldn't bear to see her daughter suffering. She agreed to move as long as Mom promised to keep Jed out of the picture. Having left Jed in New Orleans living with his brother, Mom assured Grandma that she was done with him. But it wasn't long before Mom's addiction to Jed proved once again to be stronger than her promise--even to her aging mother. Jed eventually moved back to Ohio and manipulated his way back into my mother's life.

Because they were divorced, Mom remarried Jed because her pastor said they were living in sin. Poor Grandma didn't have a chance: Once again, she was stuck in that depressing environment with Jed, who didn't work and just lolled around all day smoking pot. I tried my best to not let it come between Mom and me or Grandma and me, even though I continued to wrestle with the fact that Mom was basically using Grandma for her social security check to support Jed's lazy ass.

Doing what I believed was expected of me as the pastor-counselor I'd become to my family, I also began reaching out to build a connection with Jed as well. Although my interactions with Jed never felt right, I fed on the praise and doting I began to receive from him.

Feeling respected and appreciated by my family was an evasive prize I'd chased all my life. Not yet fully realizing that I was only taking advantage of a twisted opportunity which came to me as a result of so much dysfunction, I stepped into my new leadership role with great pride. In their eyes, I was now "somebody."

It was so hard for me to let go, knowing I was about to lose the positon I'd been elevated to for so many years in the eyes of my family, but I knew it was time to be honest. Just as I'd done several years before as a freshman in college, I picked up the phone in this small town in Mississippi to make things right.

I spoke with my sister first. She wasn't a churchgoer, so I knew she'd be the easiest to talk to and most likely the least judgmental. We laughed at the fact that it had taken me so long to talk to her about the struggles with my sexuality, when all along one of her closest friends was a lesbian. She made it clear to me that she didn't care whether I'm gay or not, although we both recognized that Mom and Grandma would feel differently.

I opened up to Mom about it the next day. As I poured out to her all the details of the life I'd been living since my separation and divorce from Andrea, her response was unexpectedly very loving and kind. I asked her if she ever worried about my being gay. She readily admitted that she'd feared it when I was young, but forgot about it once I started dating girls more seriously. She agreed to tell Grandma and Jed separately about the details of our conversation. Grandma called me to talk about it shortly after.

During the many phone calls I had with my family, I tried my best to comfort them with the fact that I was staying with the Bianchis, who believed I could change this unwanted part of myself and be restored to full-time ministry. Obviously, I must have missed something along the way trying to work through it on my own. I encouraged them that Robert, who would be leading me through the "restoration process," had already given me several books to read. Maybe something in them would provide me the solution. Even in my deep pain, I guess I couldn't let go of the responsibility I felt to take care of my family.

Not long after I arrived at the Bianchis', Viola asked me if I knew that the previous worship director of the Institute where Andrea and I'd taught had suddenly stepped down after I left. She said Andrea was temporarily given the position during the interim period. Her responsibilities included producing and serving as the main worship leader on the annual worship album. With the international platform it provided, this was one of the biggest honors at the Institute.

I could feel the anger towards Andrea's hypocrisy flood my body when Viola played for me one of the songs on the album.

This new information only reinforced what I'd suspected all along would happen after I left Andrea: She would lie and completely play the martyr, refusing to take any responsibility for our failed marriage.

Having served on the faculty at this conservative Christian organization for several years, I knew it was unconceivable for the strict authorities to allow Andrea to return to such a high-profile position, that is, unless she had lied. I'm sure it also helped her cause that her best friend was the wife of the director of the Institute.

My theory was further substantiated when I contacted the organization through which Andrea and I maintained our ministry credentials when we were together. They informed me that Andrea had reported to them that she and I had enjoyed a solid marriage without any problems. She said she was confused and in the dark as to why I would have left, but wondered if it had something to do with the pain medicine I'd been taking after my back surgery.

What she conveniently failed to tell them was that we fought constant-ly. I told her on several occasions while we were still together that if we could not get on the same page, we were going to have to step down from public ministry until we could bring our marriage under control. We had problems all right, and multiple blow-ups over the phone even after I left. The more I thought about it, I could feel all the anger I still carried for her festering daily.

When I finally got alone and quieted my bitter, screaming mind in prayer, I could hear a gentle voice ask me, "Shawn, what good is all this information doing you now? Does it really matter? Andrea has moved on with her life; are you willing to do the same?" As I felt the hardness in my heart began to soften, I asked God to help me surrender.

I knew from experience the danger in carrying anger and bitterness. It's like a cancer that destroys everything healthy; but I also knew the incredible freedom and healing found in forgiveness. So as I sat there alone in prayer in the empty church sanctuary that evening, I let it go and I forgave her.

Now it was time for me to deal with my part. I decided the best way to go about it was to write to Andrea. I knew if I were going to do this the right way, I needed to focus only on the part I played and the hurt I caused. Robert agreed to look over my letter before I sent it to make sure I was communicating effectively.

As I wrote the letter in the corner of the public library one evening, I opened up to Andrea about the deep struggles I'd had with my sexuality all my life. I assured her that my struggles had nothing to do with her. It wasn't because she wasn't pretty enough, or kind enough, or even loving enough. It was all *my* stuff—my self-hatred and hidden torment. Although it was incredibly humiliating for me to write it down, I also confessed and asked her forgiveness for the sexual infidelities I'd had with the guy I met in the park. I could have kept it to myself and she probably would've never known, but I believed it was the right thing to do. In the middle of the second floor of the old public library, my eyes unexpectedly filled with tears as I put myself in Andrea's shoes for the first time, imagining how painful our marriage must've been *for her*.

I was fortunate to receive a letter back from her not long after I mailed mine. She admitted that we both played a part in the demise of our marriage and she assured me that she forgave me. By simply allowing myself to feel some of her pain, I never felt any bitterness or anger towards her again. Our hurtful marriage had caused much damage to us both, and ironically, it was pain that opened the door to our healing.

Over the months I stayed with the Bianchis, I reached out to make amends to several people who had been hurt by me when I'd abruptly fled my life years before. For the most part, people were very loving and forgiving. Some of them were even happy to hear from me. One of the previous ministry mentors I contacted said he believed homosexuality was the most difficult stronghold to break. He said he would pray for me, but from his years of experience, most people were never able to stay free. I didn't feel very hopeful after that conversation and the more I thought about it, my doubts only multiplied.

What if I were trying to change something God never intended to be removed to begin with? What if the stronghold people thought needed to be conquered was God's doing all along? If that were the case, wouldn't I actually be fighting against God?

I eventually talked very openly to Mom about my struggling thoughts and growing skepticism over whether I could actually change my sexuality. She told me she would always love me no matter what, but my sister told me that during a conversation she had with Mom, Mom said she would never accept my being gay. She and Grandma both believed it to be sinful, and something God demanded to be changed.

To me, they were strongly reinforcing the same message I'd been tormented with since I was a boy: *God's love is unconditional— unless you're gay.*

When Joshua and Lauren moved to Nashville for Lauren to begin working on her graduate degree in nursing, the deep depression I'd temporarily risen above returned with a vengeance. I slept often and lost all desire to get out of bed in the morning. Without the fun-loving interaction of my new sidekicks to distract me, the heaviness of my circumstances outweighed every ounce of my joy.

While Robert and Viola were away in Nashville with Joshua's parents helping Joshua and Lauren find an apartment, I decided to sneak off to New Orleans for the night to medicate my pain with alcohol and sex. When Robert found out, he was so unhappy with me, and adamantly expressed that it could never happen again.

The combination of sleeping so much, moving too little, and the mounting stress I was under aggravated my back pain. There were days that I could barely walk and the fears of being sentenced to a wheelchair plagued me again. With my chronic back issues, exercising for me was never going to be an option, but I had to get moving!

I knew from experience that exercise would help alleviate my back pain as well as my depression. If I didn't exercise, I was going to wither. The only motivation I had was the misery I was in, and the unusual bond I had to this strange thing called resilience, which kept driving me forward all my life.

I used a credit card to join a local gym close to the Bianchis' home and started to exercise almost daily. It didn't take long before my back pain started to diminish right along with the dark cloud I was under.

During one of my times exercising at the gym, I recalled being enamored with a certain personal trainer at the fitness facility where Matt and I had been members in San Diego. It wasn't his handsome looks (although he was handsome) that I was drawn to, but the unusual way he interacted and cared for his clients. He acted as though no one else mattered except the person in front of him. His behavior was the polar opposite of the other trainers I saw; they were constantly flirting with others and talking or texting on their phones.

I remembered thinking, *"What this trainer is doing is just as much a ministry as what I did behind the pulpit. He's helping others to better their lives and move forward. He just uses a different platform."*

I was beginning to see that wellness was a very practical and personal way to minister to the whole person—mind, body, and spirit. *"Maybe this is something I could do!"* I thought, as I felt something stir within me. With the inward excitement continuing to grow, I could also see it serving as a perfect new opportunity to utilize my talent for public speaking, which was being wasted behind a desk.

As soon as I shared this new possibility with Matt later that evening, he quickly quenched it, accusing me of just wanting to do it to sleep with other guys.

Now, as I sat on the rowing machine in the small gym in Gulfport reliving this inspiring story, I felt that stirring sensation again. *"Maybe a part-time career in fitness would be good for me for a while!"* I thought to myself. *"Everyone has a different idea about the 'restoration process'. It's hard to know how long it will be before they allow me to return to fulltime ministry."*

I began thinking about the huge disconnect in caring for our bodies which exists in the church world, where food is the accepted drug of choice. Doesn't the Bible say that our body is the temple of God's Spirit? How is it, then, that we are often more focused on building grand structures than we are in taking care of the one true temple of God?

The next day, Robert wore a noticeable scowl on his face as I shared my idea about a part-time career in fitness. He said, "Shawn, I'm sorry, but the temptation for you would be too great."

Once again, I tucked the idea away, although I still felt compelled to study fitness and nutrition on my own time, which I did shortly after I began working part-time for a female attorney in Biloxi who attended the church Robert pastored.

Soon after Joshua and Lauren left, I started to form an unlikely bond with Robert's wife, Viola. Like an inquisitive, innocent child who asks too many questions about everything, Viola's endless curiosity at first seemed annoying to me. It wasn't until her gift of gab, along with her

enormous nurturing heart, took on a whole new meaning, as she began to peel back some of the layers of my complicated heart.

She and I often had extended conversations as I helped her paint and
redecorate the guest room. On several other occasions, she sat up
with me in the living room late into the night, listening, asking questions, and even at times crying with me. I think she was the first person
who just allowed me to talk about some of the pain of my childhood
without trying to stop me because it was too difficult to hear or feeling
the need to fix it.

As far as my being gay, Viola often told me, "Shawn, I know you think
that you're 'that way', but you're not. God did not make you like that.
It's all a lie."

I knew she meant well, but she made it sound soooo simple. She,
like many others, didn't seem to realize that there's not a gay-straight
switch to simply turn on or off.

A few months later, the Bianchis planned to go Nashville again to visit
Joshua and Lauren. They decided it would be safer this time to take
me with them. Lauren also requested that I come so I could give her
some decorating ideas for their apartment.

The day after we arrived, Joshua and I were in their living room listening to music while we all waited for a friend of theirs to arrive for lunch.
Brandon, a talented singer-songwriter, was a sophomore studying music at Belmont University. He was originally from Gulfport, where he
had been involved in the Bianchis' church. Robert was excited about
seeing him because he'd mentored Brandon for a few years before he
went off to college.

When Brandon arrived and everyone was greeting him, something alarming happened: We locked eyes—in the *gay way!* There was an immediate and undeniable attraction between us.

What started out as some innocent flirting soon turned into a heated affair when Brandon returned to Gulfport to visit one weekend. This handsome son of a wealthy doctor and I had sex all over his parents' massive beachfront home.

After Brandon went back to Nashville, we secretly spoke on the phone almost every night when I would conveniently go on my long walks to the park. I prematurely and frivolously said so many things I shouldn't have to Brandon. Part of me felt so guilty about what I was doing and the way I was deceiving the Bianchis, but the deep exhilaration I felt from new love became a welcome barrier between me and all my pain. I was in such a state of confusion, laced with elation.

When I first arrived in Gulfport and began working with Robert on my restoration process, I made it clear from the beginning that the only thing that was off the table for me was remarrying Andrea. To me, our marriage should have never happened. So when Robert asked me one day during one of our weekly counseling sessions to begin praying for God to restore my marriage to Andrea, I was furious. Even though I reminded him about our previous conversation, he seemed unwilling to take no for an answer. I felt deceived, as if he'd planned this all along through some hidden agenda.

From that moment on, I no longer trusted Robert. A few weeks later, I met Brandon in Nashville. I didn't fully understand what I was doing at the time, and poor Brandon unknowingly walked into my life at the perfect juncture to medicate me.

In the midst of all of this, I also began reconnecting by phone with some of my old friends in Houston. A few of them said they would provide me a place to stay and help me find a job if I wanted to return. When I shared this with Brandon, he said he if I were going back to Texas, he would transfer to a college in Austin in order to be closer to me. However, I knew deep down that I was in no shape to be in a serious relationship with him, nor with anyone else.

As I'd done before, I took the cowardly way out and left town while the Bianchis were away for a few days after Christmas. I met with Brandon the day I left and broke his heart as gently as I could. I trusted that he would one day understand and be grateful that I'd let him go.

I'd stayed with several families throughout my life, but I'd never felt as cared for as I did with the Bianchis. It ripped my heart out to think I would probably never see them again. Part of me wanted so badly to be the Shawn of their dreams, but I didn't know how.

CHAPTER 12

————— ❦ —————

I WENT TO the gym early Monday morning to squeeze in a quick work-out before heading off to the new fitness facility where I'd just begun working. As I completed my last two remaining exercises and walked toward the stretching area to finish up, there he was—the guy who, in the course of one drunken night, had changed my life forever. He stood only ten feet in front of me with his trainer, seemingly unaware of my presence. My pulse rate soared as beads of sweat gathered on my forehead and slowly began to trickle down my left cheek. I wanted to run, but my body had been hijacked by the traumatic memories, flipping through my mind like a Rolodex: the weeks he'd relentlessly pursued me after I returned to Houston from Mississippi, watching me, waiting for the right time; the sound of his voice whispering that he'd longed to be with me; my body lying chemically paralyzed beneath him.

"Does he have any idea of the immense pain he caused me?" I wondered. Did he know I'd quit my job shortly after what had happened, tormented for weeks on end, wanting to quit my life, too? Surely, he was completely oblivious to how I'd blamed myself for being drunk and alone that night. The crippling guilt that wracked my soul for being so naïve to take the substance he said would sober me up and make me feel better. He could never possibly know what it was like for me the day I went to the clinic to be tested and to find that I was now HIV positive.

As soon as I regained control of myself, I quickly made my way to the locker room unnoticed, changed clothes, left the gym as quickly as possible. I wanted so badly just to forget it all, but how could I do that, when there was so much to remember?

I could still see vividly in my mind's eye that late afternoon several years before as I pulled up to the front of the small café. Caleb waved at me from the patio where he'd already been seated. Even though we were roommates, we still enjoyed meeting for lunch now and then, just to catch up with the drama in each other's busy lives. Caleb was finishing up law school, and I was working as the promotions director for an upscale lounge which was owned by a gay couple, friends of the attorney for whom I'd previously worked. I enjoyed the creative side of my job, which allowed me to start a musical-theater night, bringing in live performers from the many theaters around Houston. However, I absolutely despised the tall, arrogant man who was my boss. My plan was to keep the job only as long as necessary until I could obtain a credible personal-trainer certification and pursue a new career in fitness.

It didn't take long for me to let go of all the stress I was currently under working for Mr. Never Goodenough when Caleb's dry sense of humor kicked in. His quick wit was one of things I loved most about him. After we finished eating, we continued to talk since I had the rest of the day off. I'd never told Caleb what happened to me several months before on that terrible night when I was found drunk and alone by that predator.

I felt so much shame from what had happened and decided to only tell the guy I was dating at the time. I didn't want him to hear about it from anyone else if my attacker decided to brag about his conquest. I cried as he held me the day after it happened, trying to assure me that it wasn't my fault. My boyfriend was from a very influential family and called and threatened the guy, telling him that if he ever came around me again, there would be consequences to pay. The guy completely denied any wrongdoing, and why wouldn't he? I was the perfect victim because deep down, I truly believed that I had only myself to blame.

As Caleb and I continued chatting that afternoon at the café, I felt my stomach turn when he casually brought up the guy's name while telling me a story. But it was when he said, "I don't think many people know this guy is HIV positive," that everything went dark. I tried my best to keep my composure and not allow my roommate to see my distress, but all I could think about was rushing to the clinic in Montrose to get tested.

Before the nurse said a word, I knew. His face said it all. I couldn't move. I couldn't breathe. I wanted to disappear. The first thought that eventually pierced the deafening numbness that had overtaken my mind was, *"Shawn, God's judgment has finally caught up to you."*

I sat in my car for what seemed like hours and cried until there was nothing left. Eventually, I called my friend Tommy and he came to pick me up. Later that evening, I went to see my doctor, a personal friend, at his home. He and his partner tried their best to comfort me, but the trauma of it all prevented me from hearing anything they said. I kept envisioning what Tom Hanks looked like in the movie *Philadelphia*: pale, thin, weak, and aged beyond his years. I was so uneducated on the issue, and although my doctor assured me that a positive HIV diagnosis was no longer a death sentence, it felt like one.

I tried my best to digest all that had happened to me and hold it together, but a few weeks later, when my boss once gain degraded me in his usual cynical, condescending way, something inside me snapped. Without warning, I basically gave my unsuspecting boss a private performance of the well-known country song, "Take This Job and Shove It!" Somewhat enjoying his look of complete shock at what had rolled out of sweet, people-pleasing Shawn's mouth, I went to my desk, collected my things, and stomped out in a way that would've made Johnny Paycheck proud.

Just two days before, I was informed that I'd finally be receiving a settlement from the car accident I'd had before I moved to San Diego. I'm sure the settlement, layered with my daunting diagnosis, had something to do with my new cocky attitude. I could take care of myself! But the truth was, I couldn't. I really didn't know how.

Soon after walking out of my job, I locked myself in my room for days, tormented by my thoughts:

"I walked away from everything years ago to find love and now I'll never have it."

"Who would possibly want to be with me now?"

"God, if this HIV is your judgement against me, please just take me in my sleep."

"I don't want to live anymore. Maybe I should just end it."

It seemed as though this dark pit of hopelessness that surrounded me would swallow me whole. I felt unclean, like a leper without a cure; broken, without ever being able to be put back together again. I was already living life buried under a mound of unresolved religious and childhood toxic shame, still not convinced that being gay was okay.

The added shame of my HIV diagnosis made my burden unbearable. It created the perfect storm, driving me toward my own self destruction.

My doctor told me that night at his home I would go through all the stages of grief. However, instead of cycling through each one, I found myself stuck in the denial mode. Because the HIV virus was minimal in my bloodstream at the time of my diagnosis (probably because of a weaker strain), my doctor said I could possibly hold off on starting medication for a few years. I twisted this information to my advantage in hiding from the truth, rooted in my denial. To further remove myself from reality, I told only a few people about my diagnosis. I decided if being able to *feel* hurt this much, I didn't want to feel anymore. As the weeks followed, I began to abuse alcohol and other substances to medicate my pain and help me forget.

Even though I was going down fast, I somehow managed to pull it together long enough to complete the course for my personal-training certification, and was among only a few in my class who passed the three-hour examination the first time around. I also lucked out by having already secured a job; it was being held for me until I finished my certification. The following night while I was out at a gay club celebrating my achievement, an attorney friend of mine approached me while I was standing in line for another drink. After greeting me with a hug, he leaned in and whispered in my ear, "Shawn, I heard what happened to you. Buddy, I'm so sorry! If you'll let me, I want to help you nail the fucker. I know for a fact he's done the same thing to two other guys as well."

For a moment, I just stood there. I didn't know what to say. I was too afraid to actually admit to my friend that I had HIV. I'm sure my hesitation spoke for itself, but I said, "I'm not sure what you're talking about. You must have heard some wrong information." He gently put his arm around me and kindly said, "Shawn, something tells me you're completely in denial. You were drugged and raped by that asshole. I completely understand if you don't want to talk about it now, but if you change your mind, you know where to find me. I really want to help you."

He was right: I still hadn't wrapped my head around the fact that I'd been raped. After that sobering exchange, I couldn't drink my Cape Cod fast enough.

I no longer saw myself as who I'd been before. The part of me who had been a pastor and led thousands of people in worship had been boxed up and hidden away. I didn't see him and I definitely didn't feel like him.

Feeling completely undesirable, I lived in fear that I would never find true love and that my prospects would forever be minimal because I had HIV. It was in this defeated state of mind that I began dating Enrique, a handsome, athletic college student from South America who had come to the U.S. to start a new life for himself.

Enrique was also trying to escape the pain of his past and of his wealthy, judgmental family who kicked him out and disowned him because he was gay. Neither of us was emotionally healthy enough to be in a romantic relationship, so when we began to date, it didn't take long before we both clung to each other in a very dysfunctional and co-dependent way.

My friends advised me to hold off telling Enrique about my HIV status, even though we were already having sex, until I knew for sure that things were going to become more serious between us. I knew my friends were just trying to protect me and help me feel safe; however,

I couldn't escape the gnawing fact that what was safe for me was not necessarily safe for Enrique. I continued to rationalize not telling him because the way we were having sex was much safer for him and the amount of the virus was still low in my bloodstream. I also reasoned that he actually never asked me about my HIV status; he just assumed that I was negative. Still, the growing guilt plagued me, and the longer I waited to tell him, the more difficult it became.

Our sexual relations achieved an entirely new level one particular weekend when Enrique and I were introduced to crystal meth at a party. When I first used meth, I could forget about the HIV and surrounding shame that was crushing the life out of me. It made me feel sensual and strong. Without question, the drug had the same mind-altering effect on Enrique, and it suddenly became apparent to us both why meth is such a prevalent recreational drug in the gay community. It temporarily heightened everything: our feelings about life, our feelings about each other, and definitely our feelings about sex. But the more we used it, the more we wanted it, and the riskier sex became. One of the most damaging side effects of meth is that it removes all inhibitions and with that, the ability to discern consequences. It didn't take long until this insatiable monster chained us to itself, pulling us back into its clutches without warning.

Ironically, the guy who had knowingly infected me with HIV (who continually denied being positive until much later) was the one who ended up telling Enrique of my status. I guess it was his demented way of getting back at me for telling others what he had done to me. Enrique was furious with me, as he had every right to be. What I did was inexcusable and I hated myself for it. I paid to take him to a doctor the next day with some of the settlement money I'd received, and agreed to pay whatever necessary to obtain his test results as quickly as possible. We were both greatly relieved when his test results came back negative. Enrique and I should have accepted our losses between us and ended things then and there, but our bleeding co-dependent hearts and shared love for meth held us together.

A year later on a Friday night, Enrique and I were drinking with a few friends at our small apartment. After taking a hit of Ecstasy, Enrique and I told our friends that we were going to the store and would be right back. Instead, we drove off looking for meth at the most convenient place we knew we could find it: the bath house. Once meth was in our body, all logic and sound reasoning were gone. Also gone was the ability to keep track of time. What started off as a quick trip to the store ended with our friends not hearing from us for several days. Full of worry and fear that something horrible had happened to us, someone filed a missing person's report at the police station. They also distributed flyers with a picture of me and a description of Enrique.

When we decided to resurface from our dungeon of debauchery, we found a laundry list of damages which took time and effort to clean up; in addition, we had to deal with the complete embarrassment and humiliation we had brought on ourselves and our friends. Enrique and I deceived ourselves for a long time into thinking that we didn't have a problem, since we were only "recreational users." However, reality told the story of our complete irresponsibility and the fact that we tried and tried to stop but couldn't. Over time, the days that followed each use enveloped me in a darkness greater than I'd ever known. We slowly, unknowingly became slaves to this tyrant that wanted nothing less than to destroy our lives. I felt as though the drug was creating a hole in my soul that could not be repaired, one from which my very essence was slowly draining out.

I remember leaving work one day after yet another heavy weekend of partying. As I dragged my tired body, still coming down from the drug, to my car, a well-known Bible story popped into my mind. It was from the parable of the prodigal son. In the story, the son went to his wealthy father and begged him to give him his inheritance early. Deeply grieved, the reluctant father did so. The son didn't waste any time. He packed up his things and traveled to a faraway land to live it up. There he partied away his inheritance with his friends until it was entirely gone—just as I had done with my insurance settlement.

When the son's friends realized that he was broke, they quickly deserted him. Unable to feed himself, he took a job with a pig farmer, which for a Jewish man was worse than rock bottom. As the story unfolds, one day while in the pig pen, the son comes to his senses and sees the condition he's living in. Similarly, all of a sudden it hit me: I could SEE! I, too, was living in a pig pen! My life was an unmanageable mess. I sat in my car thinking about my circumstances with tears streaming down my face. How had I allowed my life to get to this place? It was as though I didn't even realize how bad it actually was until that very moment; like I was living life in a cloud of deception that had just been pierced by a ray of sunlight. I had a college education. I'd served as a spiritual leader, taught college courses, and traveled internationally. Now I was living in a tiny apartment, could barely afford to buy food, and was about to lose my car. There in the gym parking lot, not caring if anyone saw me or not, I asked God to help rescue me out of this deep pit of darkness that my life had become.

Shortly after my spiritual awakening in the parking lot, I was determined that just like the prodigal son, I was going to do whatever it took to get my life back on track.

I soon sought out a therapist made available to me through a grant because of my HIV status. And although it broke my heart and his, I eventually ended my relationship with Enrique. I knew in my heart that as long as we stayed together, we wouldn't be able to get the help we needed. We loved each other, but we had become each other's worst enemies and strongest impediments to getting sober. I'd heard it said many times that things often get worse before they get better; this assuredly rang true.

A few months into my therapy, some major problems began to surface. My therapist Lonnie expressed to me that she didn't think I had a problem with drugs. She said I just needed to scale down my use a bit. I quickly discovered that Lonnie wasn't able to be genuinely honest with me about my issues because of the crippling guilt she carried concerning her own. Joining her at a party one night where she eventually became so intoxicated that she had to be carried out gave me enough evidence to recognize that something was terribly wrong. However, that was only the first of several times I witnessed such behavior from her. The friendship we established outside of her office had completely crossed professional boundaries and I realized I had to make some difficult decisions in order to get the help I needed. I was also greatly concerned for Lonnie's personal welfare. I decided that in my next session, I would discontinue my therapy and confront Lonnie about her own addiction and encourage her to seek some professional help as well. But as it will, life got in the way. I had to postpone my session with her until the following week.

Three days later, I received a phone call from a mutual friend telling me that Lonnie had been taken to jail on her third DUI charge, having been stopped on her way home from work. Probably knowing that she was about to be charged with a felony and would lose her credentials, she had hung herself in the holding cell. I beat myself up for a long for time over my missed opportunity to help my friend. If only I could have shared with her my concern! Why did I reschedule that damn session?! The timing of it all is something I will never understand. While still mourning the loss of my therapist and friend, I received another call a few days later. My friend Kyle, with whom I'd partied on several occasions and who had given me part-time work at his hospitality company during some difficult times, had been found hanging in his home. I went completely numb.

For weeks, I only went to work and isolated myself in my little apartment. I knew my life would most likely end the same way as Lonnie's and Kyle's if I didn't make some concrete changes. I tried using more self-control and was able to stop using drugs and alcohol for a short time, but it didn't last. After a few months, the greedy monster of addiction jerked my chain and I was once again worshiping at its feet. I found myself once again caught in the vicious cycle of using and recovering over and over. Sometimes, I partied as much as three weekends a month, from which I would often require a week to fully recover. I don't know how I was able to keep showing up for my clients with a smile on my face, but I did. When I wasn't working or partying, I was sleeping, trying to clear my head from the effects of the meth.

Eventually, I could no longer hide the considerable damage I was doing to my already struggling immune system as my once-muscular physique melted away week by week. I moved out of my small apartment and shared a house with one of my closest friends, Maria. Even though Maria had her own issues with alcohol, she was completely unaware of my drug use. I somehow kept it hidden from almost everyone around me. Of course, I was a master at hiding things about myself; I'd done it all my life. I desperately hoped that just having a roommate who didn't use meth would be enough to keep me away from it. Like most things surrounding the hidden parts of me, I was deceived.

The degree of my self-degradation hit me full force one night when I saw the pain and fear on the face of this sweet girl I cared for so deeply. Once again, I'd been partying all weekend in various places and hadn't slept for days. I ended up at a house in a sketchy, unfamiliar neighborhood. The combination of too many drugs and too little sleep catapulted me into a paranoid frenzy. I had to get out of there! I grabbed my things, left my car, and started running like a crazy man. I ran and ran, hiding behind bushes from imaginary people who were chasing me, trying to find my way home. I finally ended up at a gas station where I was able to gain some composure long enough to ask the attendant to call me a taxi. During my frenzy, I'd also called Maria and left her several fragmented messages about my need for a ride and the part of town where I was lost. After several vain attempts to return my calls, she decided to go out looking for me.

Maria's brother had warned her that the part of town I was lost in was very dangerous and that she shouldn't go. All she could think about was my being out there alone and lost, so she came anyway. Terribly afraid and unable to find me, she went back home, hoping I would eventually show up. Not long after, the taxi dropped me off and I quickly made my way into the house. I will never forget the look on Maria's face. She had always respected and looked up to me as someone she could count and rely on. The person who came through the door was not the Shawn she knew, but some cracked-out shell of a man who greatly frightened her.

The following day my friend Ashley, a brilliant entrepreneur to whom I'd grown close, came by to take me looking for my car. She, like Maria, had no clue that I'd been using drugs and was obviously having a difficult time digesting this new information about her friend. The disappointment and confusion I saw in her eyes was almost too much for me to bear at that point. After we found my car and she led me back to my house, she pleaded with me to do whatever I had to do to get help. I promised her I would.

Throughout my life I'd been surrounded by friends and acquaintances I witnessed reaching out to their parents and family when they were in distress. *"What would it feel like?"* I often wondered, just to know the option was there to pick up the phone and say, "Dad, I'm in trouble. Can you help me?" or "Mom, I'm really hurting; what should I do?" Having that kind of family support system was something I'd never been able to relate to. And although I often tried my best to show how happy I was for the good fortune of my friends who did have loving families, I always grieved a little for myself.

There is a section of scripture in the New Testament that talks about being adopted into the family of God through Christ. It says that once this heavenly adoption takes place, God the Father from then on calls us sons and daughters. One evening while I was studying this passage in the Bible college library, it was as though God was using it to speak directly to me. I suddenly realized that I'd carried a lot of hidden anger and resentment toward God for years, over the fact that I'd cried out to Him night after night when I was a boy, begging for a loving family to adopt me. As a child, it seemed like a simple request, knowing that He was God and my family didn't want me. But no one ever came to rescue me, and my suffering continued.

As I sat in the library with my head propped up between both of my hands, fervently looking down at my Bible, I could hear in my heart God saying, "My son, I never sent another family to adopt you when you were little because I wanted to adopt you for my own." When I inwardly heard God call me His son, the healing tears began to flow, and I couldn't get out of the library fast enough.

Even though I'd had this spiritual experience which greatly impacted me back in Bible college, the fear of constantly waiting for the next disaster kept me in a state of dread—that gnawing feeling of spending life on the edge of a mountain with no safety net to catch me if I slipped. Throughout the years, I tried my best to comfort myself in the belief that my Father God would catch me if I fell. But at the same time, I also couldn't seem to shake the inner longing for a human someone who simply had my back. It was an inner tormenting contradiction.

When Ashley left that afternoon after helping me find my car, all I could think about was reaching up to my Heavenly Father like a hurting child and crawling up on His lap for protection and comfort. I picked up my Bible and held it tightly as I lay on my bedroom floor and cried myself to sleep.

Enrique and I were very kind and loving to each other as we met for lunch close to downtown that Wednesday afternoon. It was the first time I'd seen him in over nine months. He had put some weight back on and looked much better. We both did. I'd moved in to my own apartment shortly after the night I scared my poor friend Maria with my craziness. I couldn't bear the thought of hurting her like that again. After Enrique and I lightened up the heavy atmosphere with a little laughter, I grabbed his hand and told him how sorry I was for any pain I'd caused him. He opened up to me as well, sharing with me how he hated me for a while after breaking up with him like I did, but now he understood why I had to. He also told me he was sorry for the way he hurt me by using my HIV status to put me down.

When I told him that I'd started going back to church again and was going to start weekly counseling with a minister to try and change my sexuality, he laughed, saying in his thick Spanish accent, "Shawn, you're *gay!*"

I smiled back at him and said, "Who knows? Maybe one day I'll even marry a woman again!"

With that, Enrique laughed even harder.

CHAPTER 14

---◌◌---

I FELT A warm, unexpected arm around my left shoulder as I knelt down at the expansive altar in the front of the megachurch on the south side of Houston. Feeling a bit intimidated inside the ten-thousand-seat auditorium, I felt comforted to have someone beside me. As I looked up with tear-filled eyes, I saw a familiar smiling face framed by edgy, spiked black hair; it was Jeffrey, one of the pastors! His was not a common look for someone in Houston, Texas, and even less common for a pastor. I recognized him instantly, having seen him several times leading worship on the massive stage with his pretty wife Kaela. With her own pink-tipped hair and punk-rocker style, she, like her husband, seemed out of place in such a conservative environment. The fact that they didn't look like they fit in consoled me, as I sported my California-style highlighted hair and muscular physique.

As the service ended and Jeffrey and I continued to stand in front of the stage talking, Kaela walked up front to meet me. "Kaela, this is Shawn," Jeffrey said.

"Hi, Shawn," she responded, holding out her hand to shake mine, beaming a friendly smile.

"Shawn used to be in ministry and has recently come back to the Lord," Jeffrey added. "He's friends with Timothy Crandall."

"Really?!" she responded, with heightened interest. "How do you know him?"

I explained to her that Timothy and I had been close friends years before while working together at the institute in Dallas. "Timothy's actually the one who suggested that I check out this church," I added.

"Timothy's pretty big-time now in worship music, isn't he?" Kaela asked candidly.

"Is he?" I asked, feeling a little embarrassed that I didn't know this already (especially since Tim and I had been talking on the phone weekly at that point).

"Well, yeah!" she said, laughing slightly. "Where have you been?! The last few worship albums he's put out with his church are some of the hottest ones on the market. We sing several of his songs here. Do you know Kati, the girl who sings with him, the one he's now managing? She's starting to become even bigger than he is. Although, person-ally, I don't get it, with her one-octave range," Kaela added.

I did know who Kaela was talking about, although I didn't realize Kati was now working with Tim. She was also a graduate of the institute where Tim and I had taught. I'd heard her sing on one of the school's worship albums a friend had sent me after I'd left. I agreed that she didn't have as great a voice as some of the others who had sung at the school over the years, but more important than that, she possessed an undeniably strong anointing—a characteristic I'd always believed was much rarer. Of course, I never said anything, afraid it would sound too egotistical with her rising popularity, but something in me related with her. I clearly recognized when I was in ministry that I never had as polished a voice as many of the others around me. I was often

Thorns of Chester Street

discouraged with deep regret how I'd wasted the opportunity when I was in college to train and develop my voice to its full potential. But what I didn't have in skill, God seemed to make up for with the anointing He'd given me. I knew this only because of what others told me and how the crowds responded when I sang. It always humbled me, because deep down, I knew the responses of others when I led worship had little to do with me.

Jeffrey and Kaela invited me to go with them to dinner directly after the service so I could meet a few of the other pastors. Anxious for acceptance and friendship in my new environment, I gladly accepted their invitation. Although everyone was particularly kind to me, I still felt so out of place.

Feeling the urge just to blend back in and hide from the extent of my troubles, I scheduled a time to meet with Jeffrey and Kaela the following week before I left the restaurant that night.

I met with them privately a few days later at the church and unloaded everything: my homosexuality, drugs, alcohol, and the thing I dreaded most to tell—having HIV. Their kindness and compassion drew me in even more as they assured me that everything I shared with them would remain completely confidential. I trusted them.

Just for fun, I decided to research my friend Timothy Crandall on the Internet the next day. I wanted to see what all the fuss was about. I couldn't believe all that he'd accomplished! What was even more wonderful was that the very church where he led worship, which was becoming internationally recognized for its worship music, had originally approached me about the position of worship leader just before I walked away from the church. I actually found this odd coincidence to be very meaningful, knowing that my close friend had stepped into that very position and done much more with it than I ever could have. No one I personally knew in ministry deserved the success more. Tim was one the most genuine and humble people I'd ever met. His humility is actually what drew me to him as a friend. What I loved even more about Tim's success was that he'd often been overlooked by the leadership of the institute where we had both taught. Tim did most of the work preparing the band and singers for many of the worship recordings, yet he was never given the opportunity to lead even one song on them. *"Who's laughing now?"* I thought. *"I love it when God does that!"*

After reading all of Tim's accolades, I sat in front of my computer thinking how it was just like Tim to be as busy as he was and still make time for messy me. There was no doubt my world of sex and drugs lay completely outside his comfort zone. He made a commitment to help me, and had his assistant work me into his calendar so we could talk every week at the same time. Our weekly talks provided a temporary boost to my ravaged self-esteem.

Over the coming weeks, Jeffrey and Kaela swiftly fused me into their inner circle. They were lots of fun to be around, and I occasionally spent the night at their house, where we stayed up late into the night talking about life and ministry. Obviously, they both felt very comfortable with me and unexpectedly began to open to up to me as well about some of their own personal struggles. The church had recently relocated them from a previous church position in Dallas. Jeffrey had been serving in this new position as an associate pastor in charge of worship and media for only a little over a year.

They shared that they didn't care for how legalistic their new senior pastor was, but were advised by the senior associate pastor and his wife to wait it out. The senior associate told them that once the senior pastor retired, the church administration planned on making lots of changes to soften things and make the church more "seeker friendly". The big question: How long would it be until the senior pastor retired? Jeffrey said the pastor would often speak as if it were to be soon, and then he'd completely change his tune the next time they spoke. Like the old proverb says, "Hope deferred makes the heart sick," and the frustration for Jeffrey and Kaela was clearly in the waiting.

I could recognize the legalism they were talking about, but legalism was something I'd always been oddly drawn to as well. I liked the rigid structure and sense of control it provided. I'd always despised feeling controlled by others, but with all the chaos I felt inside, believing I had the ability to somehow control something felt important—even if it was myself.

I came from a ministry background which favored complete loyalty and respect for spiritual leadership. The fact that my new friends continuously gossiped about their pastor didn't sit well with me, but even so, I tolerated it just to have a sense of belonging.

Jeffrey and Kaela were opportunists, but my deep need for acceptance inhaled the frequent compliments and attention I received from them about my physique and my knowledge of fitness. Kaela was clearly emotionally troubled and obsessive about losing weight and looking pretty. Jeffrey, with his short attention span, offset by his luring energy, also said he also wanted to lose weight and to start working out. "It can be a tradeoff," they cleverly said. "You teach us how to get in shape and we will help you." (Translation: "We'll teach you how to not be gay and not use drugs.") I soon began teaching them about healthy eating principles and I trained Jeffrey for free. I was happy and felt grateful that even in my depleted emotional state, I still had something to give that others wanted.

The complexity of my relationship with my new friends (and pastors) became even more convoluted when they took me with them one Friday night to a private house party hosted by some of their friends who did not attend the church. Sitting on the sofa, Kaela leaned in and quietly said, "Shawn, you're okay with drinking, right? Just not the other stuff."

Feeling awkward and caught off guard, I said, "Yeah, I--I'm fine with it." (Even though there was not a doubt in mind that their conservative senior pastor would *not* be.)

Just then, Jeffrey returned, holding two red plastic cups into which he'd secretly poured vodka while in the kitchen, and handed one to Kaela. "Shawn's FINE with it," she said very softly, over-enunciating the words to Jeffrey. He turned to me smiling and responded, "Oh good, I'm glad you're cool with it, bro."

But truly, the whole thing didn't feel right to me. I felt completely disappointed—and not because they were alcohol drinkers. I hadn't even bought into the fact that I had an issue with alcohol myself at that time, but what if I had? They didn't even feel the need to discuss it with me before taking me to this party. I was more disappointed that they had put me in this uncomfortable position and seemed completely clueless about it. Probably what bothered me the most was the sudden realization that if I were looking to this pastor and his wife to help me with my addictions (since the church believed that homosexuality was an addiction, just like alcohol and drugs), I was in big trouble!

"Can I get you some?" Jeffrey asked with a smirk.

"No, I'll pass, but thanks," I responded, trying really hard to hide my awkwardness.

They drank only enough that night to become very talkative, but I knew the whole thing had crossed the line. A few hours later, after we went back to their house and continued talking, the night became even more confusing when Kaela confessed how much they missed going out to the gay clubs in Dallas to dance occasionally. I never said anything, but my heart continued to sink further into disillusionment.

I relapsed with meth the following Friday. Even though it was just for the night and not the usual entire weekend as the many times before, the agony I felt was even more brutal. The self-loathing and inner turmoil I experienced felt like trying to hold onto flat, slippery walls while the sandy floor beneath me slowly disappeared into a bottomless pit.

For the rest of that weekend, I cried out to God over and over for mercy and deliverance, begging for His forgiveness and asking for more self-control.

I refused to be comforted, as though I deserved the pain, relentlessly beating myself up, as I screamed out loud, "Shawn, why are you so stupid! How could you do this again? Why are you so weak? You used to be so much stronger than this!"

Completely exhausted after hours of fighting my demons and lashing out at myself, I finally pulled myself up from the floor and onto my bed late Sunday evening. With no more fight to give in the darkness of my room, I heard a voice distinctly say, "Shawn, stop punishing yourself!"

And right then, the turmoil in my mind *stopped.*

My eyes widened as each word I heard saturated my soul with new awareness. I was able to identify how conditioned I'd been for punishment at a very young age. It was all I knew. I didn't know life without it. I was punished for not knowing how to do something right without having ever been taught; I was punished when Jed lost something and I couldn't find it; I was punished for chewing with my mouth open, for slurping with my straw, for having an opinion; I was punished for having fun, laughing, or talking too much; I was punished for acting "like a girl," being in the way, and when I was simply too afraid to be found. I was punished just for being.

Even though I said I believed and even taught others that Jesus took our punishment on the cross, I obviously didn't really believe it applied to me. I still continued to punish myself because I believed I deserved it. I'd become comfortable with punishment, and when it was absent, I felt like something substantial was missing. Continuously impaired by this contorted view of myself, I now held in my hand the whip of sex, drugs, and alcohol.

I didn't feel easy with peace and serenity, because inwardly, peace and serenity had never been a part of me.

With a newly intensified effort, I grabbed hold of the Church, Jesus, and determination more than I had in years to steady my course and change my life. Through my relationship with Jeffrey, I was able to score an appointment with the senior associate pastor (not an easy feat in a church of 15,000 members) to share with him my story and to ask for his guidance.

After I met with him, he suggested that I move closer to the church where "sin was no longer in [my] backyard." He also recommended that I meet with the man in charge of the local Exodus International group. He was a reparative therapist and led a support group there at the church every week. Eager to move forward, I agreed to follow through with both of my new pastor's proposals.

The following week, I had a private session with the reparative therapist. I found him utterly repulsive. He was arrogant and self-righteous, and did a lousy job of trying to hide either one. He made it clear that not many had the fortitude to fully make the transition from gay to straight, as he had. The fact that I could easily see his physical attraction to me made his puffed-up attitude and words fall flat on the ground. There wasn't an ounce of inspiration or encouragement in the entire session with this man. I left feeling turned off and more discouraged than ever.

As soon as my lease was up in the city, I moved closer to the church in a new subdivision in Galveston County. It was located halfway between Houston and Galveston Island. I had to wake up by 3:00 a.m. each day in order to meet my first client at 5:00 in the Houston gym where I worked as a trainer.

It was a grueling schedule, but I was resolved to do whatever it took to be obedient. My new apartment was very isolated and I was basically living out in the middle nowhere, but as I'd been instructed, the gay bars of Houston were no longer within my easy reach.

Following my friend Timothy's advice, I met with the senior associate pastor again to share my disappointing experience with the Exodus International therapist and to see if there were any other alternatives for me. He seemed surprised and quite impressed that I'd actually moved my residence, and said that he would do what he could to help me. Although he did pick up the phone to have his secretary schedule an appointment for me to meet with the associate pastor in charge of counseling, I sensed a certain pretense and homophobia from him this time around that made me feel very uneasy.

I began counseling with Pastor Bob the following week, and stayed with it for the better part of a year. With a Santa Claus physique and a jovial laugh to match, I found him to be a kind and compassionate man. He was easy to talk to and very encouraging.

I tried my best to only see Bob's heart, which was as big as the moon; however, I had a hard time with the fact that he was trying to help me gain more self-control of my addictions (because he, like the rest of the church, also believed homosexuality to be an addiction), but would often joke about and minimize his own obvious addiction to food.

I also felt badly for Bob's shaky self-esteem, which I easily recognized, and which seemed to be enhanced somehow by his interactions with the senior associate pastor. I often wondered if he might have been putting himself under a lot of pressure to "cure me" of my homosexuality just to keep his job. I began to see that the senior associate pastor was just like so many others I'd met along the way in ministry who fed on intimidating others and was driven by the need to prove something. I probably recognized the dynamic of it all much more easily because I'd been in the same place myself several times.

I'd recognized it many other times; however, the extent of pastor Bob's disconnect with my "gay circumstance" became blatantly clear to me one day when he made the comparison that gay relationships were obviously not of God because gay couples didn't really love each other as heterosexual couples did.

Although being gay was something I was still trying to change at that point, I knew from experience that Bob's comment was ridiculous and not based in reality. I challenged him on the fact that the love I experienced with Enrique in the first year of our relationship was much deeper and felt more natural than what I had ever known with my wife. I told him I'd always felt like an imposter when I was with Andrea, but that sickening feeling was completely removed when I was with Enrique, because I could relax and be my true self.

By the look on his face, it appeared as though an errant bird had flown into the hard wiring in Bob's belief system and it was about to short circuit. I'm sure my challenge to his pastoral insight must have been even more unsettling for him by that time, since we'd been working together for a while and I'd gained his respect as a spiritually grounded person.

I tried my best to shake off the many times purely ignorant comments like these were made about being gay, yet I still wasn't satisfied with the fact that so many ministers could only see being gay as something a person *did* and *chose* (an outward expression), rather than just *was*. How could I believe in what they were saying to me when it was so easy to see that they just didn't get it? Being gay incorporates far more neurons, deeper devotions, and plucks many more heartstrings than a single sexual act could ever conjure up. Being gay doesn't come from the outside; it comes from deep on the inside. One simply knows.

In all this interaction with Pastor Bob, confusion, frustration, and discouragement became even greater for me. How could Pastor Bob help me if he didn't have a realistic grasp on what it was all about?

An even bigger shocker than my friend Timothy's success came as I realized the three teenage boys of Justin Barlyn, the worship leader I used to sing with and work for at the institute, were now the biggest pop-boy-band on the planet! How did that happen without my knowing?! It only substantiated how isolated a life I'd been living during the height of my partying and drug use.

As I watched a Christmas television special with the boys touring the White House as guests of the President, I could easily remember the three of them as little tykes: the oldest, wide-eyed and animated, who made it to the final callbacks for the remake of the classic movie *Miracle on 34th Street;* the middle one, who looked the most like his mom and had to work so hard to overcome his speech impediment; and the curly-haired youngest, in diapers, making grunting sounds and pointing at everything, seemingly on his own timetable for when he'd begin to speak. The last time I'd seen them was when Andrea and I first began traveling with the worship band; we performed a concert at the church their dad was pastoring in New Jersey. I think the oldest was about ten years old at the time. It didn't even seem as though these memories were from my life anymore, but from some movie or book I'd read.

Watching their dad Justin, my old friend, and his wife being interviewed by Oprah Winfrey about managing the career of their wildly popular sons was a lot to wrap my head around. The media actually compared their popularity to the Beatles! There is no doubt where these boys got their talent or how they got their start in the music business: Their dad had the golden vocal chords of a crooner and was an equally talented songwriter and producer. Seeing him on the screen in front of me delivered a bag of mixed emotions. I'd worked very closely with him while I was a student at the institute in Dallas. Having come there with prior pastoral and worship-leading experience, Justin gave me a full scholarship to be his assistant worship leader my final year before graduating. He was in the process of founding the recording label for the institute at that time and was also teaching songwriting workshops on the side. I realized I'd been given a highly coveted opportunity and I wanted to make the most of it.

Maybe it was because he was only five years older than I, or that I was dating one of his favorite former students (the woman I loved and almost married before Andrea), but I surprisingly found myself as his confidant in just a short time. Justin often called me to walk the running track with him at night while he opened up about his life and the obstacles he faced working for the institute.

The degree to which he opened up his heart to me was humbling, and I'm sure the fact that we both knew what it was like to feel unwanted as children (his biological mother had given him to her father to raise) provided us common ground on which to connect. Since I often lived life walking on a highwire of anxiety, I coveted his cool demeanor. What Justin hadn't been given in looks was made up for tenfold with charisma. He had a rare way about him that instantly made a person feel close to him, and his sweet, soft-spoken persona made it very difficult to hold anything back from him. I wanted to open up to him about my hidden battle with my sexuality, and the deep concerns I had about hurting my girlfriend over it. However, when I happened to walk into his office one day and heard Justin engaging in homophobic humor and comments with another colleague about one of the students whom some thought to be gay, I decided it wouldn't be safe for me to confide in him about this part of myself.

Throughout my years in ministry, homophobia had an odd way of showing up in others just before I was about to become vulnerable. This phenomenon produced a dual effect: I often felt protected, yet greatly frustrated and discouraged. Holding back from opening up to this man turned out to be a wise decision, as I was eventually hurt, disappointed, and cut off from his inner circle after I broke up with my girlfriend.

Before I started getting close to Justin, I'd been warned by a few friends who'd previously worked with him to guard my heart when it came to any smooth-talking opportunities he offered, but I didn't want to hear it or believe it. But after some time, I started to see through this one I'd so admired, as the cloak of false humility slowly began to slip off, just like his empty promises. What started out as a close and meaningful friendship turned into a very uncomfortable working relationship.

Before I left the institute to begin my second pastorate position in Illinois, I scheduled an appointment with Justin. I didn't want to leave anything undone between us, so I decided that if *he* wouldn't talk with me about whatever it was that caused him to toss me to the side, *I* would talk with him about it. As I sat in his office, I was appalled that he wouldn't even acknowledge that anything had happened. For a moment, his silent response of omission made me feel foolish for even bringing it up; even so, I asked him to forgive me anyway if I'd done anything to hurt or offend him. I wanted to leave knowing I'd at least done my part to heal the divide between us. It's ironic that he left the institute not long after that because he felt that he was being unfairly treated and underappreciated by the co-founder.

Interestingly, several years later, I joined the faculty at the institute and was given Justin's old office. I called him for permission one day to use one of his songs on our first album, to which he agreed. Although he never said anything to me about what he thought of our arrangement or production of his song, it remained my favorite track on the album. Time definitely has a way of healing, and in this case with my old friend, that did for me.

In retrospect, I did have unrealistic expectations of my friend. At thirty years old, he was still a very young man when I worked with him, and it wasn't fair to him that I was the one who chose to put him on a pedestal.

CHAPTER 15

—— ♋ ——

Late one Tuesday evening, I received a phone call from my stepmother informing me that my dad's mother Fannie had passed away in Michigan. She asked if I could come to Ohio where Grandma Fannie was to be buried alongside her husband Grandpa Josef, and officiate the memorial service and graveside ceremony. I agreed to come and help in any way I could, recalling that I'd promised my grandmother just a year before during a brief visit that I would sing "Amazing Grace" at her funeral.

After I ended the phone call with my stepmother, I sat in the quiet of my minimally furnished apartment and thought about the last time I'd seen Grandma Fannie. I had just traveled to Michigan from Houston two days before to visit my dad, who was in poor health. With two back surgeries, a hip replacement, two open-heart surgeries, and a growing aortic aneurysm, it was actually a miracle that he was still living. Grandma Fannie was also in very poor health from multiple complications with diabetes, bedridden in a nursing home. She'd been in that condition for some time. Realistically, I knew there was a strong possibility that this could be the last time I'd see either one of them.

Dad had been on disability for years from a work-related accident at one of the country's leading automobile conglomerates in Saginaw. His health had continued to deteriorate, but he still did the best he could to get out and enjoy his heavily wooded property, which he loved so much. I'd not spent any quality time with Dad since I was in my early twenties, and it had been many years since I'd seen him at all.

Now as a grown man, I was shocked at how childlike my father seemed—such a stark contrast with how I remembered him. Just like Grandma Fannie, he had a needy way of completely swallowing up every conversation and making it all about him. Strangely, though, I felt no judgment this time around. I felt only empathy for him. Staying with Dad and my stepmother in their home gave me the opportunity to see him and accept him as he was, and begin the process of letting go of the unrealistic expectations I'd carried of him.

As I lay on the bed in their guest room that first night, I felt an unforeseen surge of gratefulness. Seeing and interacting with Dad allowed me to grasp the magnitude of what God had saved me from, and I knew what a miracle it was.

Before I fell asleep that night, I was reminded of the only letter my dad had ever sent me. It arrived while I was still married to Andrea, during a six-month jail sentence he was serving for multiple DUI and domestic-abuse charges. Dad's father could not read or write and Dad's writing ability was very elementary at best. Recognizing the amount of humility and the level of vulnerability it required of him to craft and send it to me made the letter even more valuable.

Shawn how the time passes, just the other day I held you for the first time you were 10 days old, I didn't know how to handle it I was only 18 years old. I tried to give you everything I could, but I forgot 1 thing love but I do love you I hope you know that, I was the one that could never show love but it was always there, I have so much to tell you but I can't find the words, but there tho. Tell your wife shes a lucky women to have you, and your sure a lucky man to have her, may God bless you both.

P.S. have a happy 29th birthday it only comes once, pray for me because I sure do you

P.S.S. don't mind the spelling I never went to school to much I grew up to fast I didn't think I would ever need it, man was I ever wrong

Love ya son

Dad

The following day, I found it very strange that Dad refused to enter Grandma Fannie's room with me when he took me to visit her in the facility where she lived. I thought it to be even stranger when she told me he'd stopped visiting her some time before. Of my grandmother's five children, my dad was clearly her favorite, and she had no qualms about letting everyone know it. She often raved about how handsome and athletic he was when he was younger. I distinctly remember how she made excuses to everyone for his poor behavior, as though he could do no wrong. I was no exception; she made the same worthless excuses to me when I was just a boy, for his chronic absence and the capacious dumpster I dragged behind me, filled with his broken promises.

When I was older, Grandma Fannie would often shame me for not calling Dad frequently enough, although he never made any effort to be a part of my life. I despised the way she would try to manipulate me when we talked on the phone. I often felt angry when she said, "But Shaawn, he's your daaad," as if that title alone gave him the right to take no responsibility for his conduct. I never had any kind of meaningful relationship with either one of them, yet I often blamed myself for not trying hard enough.

Just like Dad, Grandma was a braggart, and I recall her often boasting to me how she used to do all of Dad's homework for him when he was in high school so he could go off and have fun with his friends. Mom had told me that while she was still married to Dad, Grandma used cover up for him when he was sneaking around with other women. There were obviously many layers to Dad and Grandma Fannie's dysfunctional relationship. Maybe the special treatment she showed him was her way of trying to make up for some of the abuse he suffered at the calloused hands and heart of his own father.

Mom said she believed Grandpa Josef was mostly to blame for "messing up Dad's head" when he was young. I'd never witnessed my grandfather's anger, but I heard the stories, and my dad bore the emotional scars to prove them true.

Mom revealed that Grandpa would beat the hell out of Dad anytime he lost a fight (claiming he was training him to be a prize boxer); but when Mom also disclosed how Grandpa forced Dad to kill, skin, cook, and eat his own pet rabbit because he hadn't done his chores, I knew then the depth of abuse my poor dad had suffered. Grandpa's heartless behavior had *sociopath* written all over it. The complete horror of that story alone brought so much into perspective for me about my dad. I think what had thrown me off from the reality of it all for so many years was how Dad always bragged about Grandpa and how close they appeared. I didn't learn about the Stockholm Syndrome (in which the victim unconsciously turns the persecutor into a friend in order to survive) until many years later; this was most likely at play in their relationship. I'm sure that just as I was, Dad was also doing the best he could just to survive.

There's little doubt that Grandma Fannie, Dad, and his older sister Julia were mentally ill. Aunt Julia was a diagnosed paranoid schizophrenic who went into and out of mental institutions all her life until she passed away in her early fifties. She had a hard time with reality and would often believe she was the Virgin Mary carrying the baby Jesus. Even though she was usually heavily medicated, I loved the occasional opportunities I had to stay the night with her and my two cousins when I was young. To me, Julia was always kind and sweet. She loved seeing me dance around singing the Donna Summer hit song "Last Dance", which she requested often. Sadly, I don't recall her husband, my Uncle Edgar, being home much. He left Aunt Julia for another woman and she never seemed to fully recover from that.

Along with exhibiting sociopathic behavior just like his father, Dad also had an interesting relationship with reality. When I was young and would occasionally stay with him, he often showed me a photo album full of Polaroid pictures of dead bodies in army fatigues, lying on the side of the road with no heads and mangled limbs. He told me he had taken those pictures himself in Vietnam when he was fighting in the war. He also let me hold the Purple Heart medallion he had in his keepsake box, as well as a few other medals he said he he'd been awarded. All his adult life, he told people he was a veteran of the Vietnam War, but he'd never been to Vietnam.

Mom was married to Dad the entire time he was in the Army. She said he was stationed in Maryland and never left the United States. Mom also told me the pictures and the Purple Heart had belonged to his best friend, a black man, who was actually killed in Vietnam, and for some unknown reason Dad ended up with his things. Whether Dad's charade of adopting his friend's story and making it his own was rooted in deep shame from survivor's guilt, or it was some contorted way of keeping his friend alive, it had definitely become a part of him. His longtime girlfriend and my stepmother both told me that he would occasionally wake up in the middle of the night terrified, in a cold sweat, from a nightmare he had about himself fighting in Vietnam. Even in his sleep, his contorted mind told him he was in a place he'd never been.

While Dad was stationed in Maryland, he also fathered a daughter before returning home to Ohio to Mom and me. I was about a year old at the time. This unknown half-sister of mine, whom I'd never met or knew anything about, tracked me down many years later while I was living in Chicago. We talked for several hours on the phone one night and she told me that Dad had told her the same Vietnam story.

He'd also told my half-sister that he never knew anything about her or had any knowledge that her mother was pregnant before he left Maryland. Dad actually made her mother appear to be the liar, which created a rift between his secret daughter and her mother for a period of time. Sadly, she unknowingly stepped into the same deceptive trap I'd been caught in so many times throughout my life with Dad. I learned the hard way that whenever I spoke with my dad, I needed to be cautious: I could never be sure whether his stories were true or fictitious.

A few weeks later, after I spoke with Mom, I was able to contact my half-sister again and provide her some more accurate details. Mom readily confessed to me that she had always known I had a sibling in Maryland. She said when Dad was drinking while they were married, he would often brag about how he had gotten a few other women pregnant just to hurt her.

She related to me how Dad said he responded to my half-sister's mom when she called him to tell him she was pregnant. He said he told her, "What in the hell do you expect me to do about it; I'm getting ready to move back to Ohio with my wife and newborn son! You'll just have to get an abortion."

Mom said Dad also bragged about a third child he had supposedly fathered with a local stripper. Even though I shared this information with my newfound half-sister, I could hear in her voice that she didn't want to believe it. Completely aware of how persuasive my Dad could be, I knew where her hesitation was coming from. Unfortunately, just like I'd had to, this was something she would probably have to learn for herself.

One afternoon while I was in middle school, visiting Grandma Fannie, she offered me ten dollars along with some sort of diet pill in exchange for my cleaning her house. She said the pill was harmless for me to take and would help me clean faster. She was right about that! At only twelve years old with thanks to my grandmother, I was high on amphetamines for the first time—a stark contrast to my Mom's mother, who gave me my first Bible.

I have no idea whether Grandma Fannie had ever been treated for mental illness, although many of the signs point to bipolar disorder. She had an enormous personality and could be very persuasive when she wanted something. I'm sure all the pills and the liter of Pepsi she consumed every day only added to her grandiosity. She'd hurt her back when she was young and had been hooked on prescription pain and diet pills for years. The only time I ever saw her leave her recliner in front of the TV was to go to the bathroom or to bed.

I often overlooked her manipulative behavior because of the sadness I felt for her. Grandma's hygiene had become pretty much non-existent because of her illness and sedentary lifestyle. She resembled nothing of the beautiful red-haired Irish girl from a prosperous family heritage, standing beside her handsome husband in the old black-and-white framed picture I often stared at in her living room.

Maybe I stared at her beautiful picture because I'd never seen Grandma Fannie in that way. The picture I carried in my mind was much different: fragmented and twisted, like a Picasso. She had a grand, charismatic way of making me feel like I was the most important and special person in the world at times. At other times, I wanted to hide from her.

There was a side of Grandma that I never told anyone about: a dark, sexual side that scared me. She used to say all kinds of disgusting and vile things to me—things that should never be said to a child. Her words made me feel the same way I felt when I'd been physically molested or violated by others.

I never understood why she would do that to me, and then just laugh about it. In some sick, demented way, she seemed to enjoy seeing me squirm and be uncomfortable. Apparently, she found pleasure in the sexual things she would say to me and the questions she would ask.

Like many other unwanted parts of my childhood, the way I dealt with Grandma Fannie's sexual abuse was to box up each incident and store it away in a dark corner somewhere so no one could see.

Maybe that's why Dad didn't want to enter Grandma Fannie's room when he knew she was about to die. Maybe he, too, had boxes of painful memories of her, and the shame wouldn't allow him to risk her trying to open them up to clear her conscience before she died.

Traveling back to Ohio to stay with Mom for Grandma Fannie's funeral posed some emotional challenges. I was really glad to see Mom and her mother, but just like every other time I visited them throughout the years, I was also enrobed in a certain darkness I couldn't seem to shake. I tried my best to never let it show and never said a word about it, but it was always present. Like a familiar ghost from the past, this distressing feeling typically stayed with me for weeks even after I left.

There was also the daunting issue at hand: I'd not spoken nor sung publicly for years, and I knew that preparing a message honoring Grandma Fannie's life was not going to be an easy task. I knew I had little to say about her that was good, and the reality of that was both sad and frightening.

As I stood in front of my family at the memorial service in the funeral home, just like riding the proverbial bike, my years of ministry experience kicked in and I gave the perfect pastoral performance. I sang an updated version of "Amazing Grace" to honor Grandma's request, and I delivered a message about the person Grandma would have described herself to be (not the person she actually was).

My main objective was to help everyone *feel* better, and that's exactly what I did, even though I had completely unplugged from reality to do it. I knew that none of them wanted to hear the truth about Grandma Fannie anyway, which worked out fine for me because I certainly wasn't ready to tell it.

The best part of returning to Ohio was the precious time I was afforded with my sweet eighty-one-year-old maternal grandmother. She was so happy and relieved that I was back in church and talking about returning to the ministry. She had a small TV room in the front of the house that she shared with Mom and Jed, where we sat, talked, and watched a few old movies together. Most people would have probably found it boring to be sitting like that for hours, but I loved every minute of it. Grandma even allowed me to coax her into learning a few simple exercises that could help improve her mobility, although I knew she would probably never do them on her own.

The day before I returned to Houston while we were both looking through some old photo albums, Grandma turned to me and gently said, "Shawn, I really had no idea how bad your childhood was when you were little. I know you told me, but I didn't listen. It wasn't until I moved in with your mom and Jed that I was able to see things more clearly. I want you to know how sorry I am."

With her eyes glassy from tears, she added, "I wish so bad that I had listened to you back then. I have cried about it and asked God to forgive me over and over. To think, I could have saved you from so much pain. If I got to do it all over again, sweetheart, I would have taken you away from them and raised you myself! Grandma loves you so much. You were such a sweet little boy and I loved you just like you were my own son. I had a special bond with you that I've never had with anyone else. You know that, don't you?"

"Yes, Grandma, I know that," I said with a smile. "Thank you for saying this to me," I said lovingly, as I reached out to hold her hand across the end table. "It means more to me than you can know."

After several minutes of silence, Grandma said, "You know, Shawn, I've never told this to anyone else before, but when I was a young girl, my mother had to send me and my brother to stay with my favorite aunt and uncle when she was going through a hard time. One night, when no one else was home, my uncle called me into his bedroom and molested me. I was so ashamed and so hurt that he would do that to me. I felt so dirty when that happened, and I never wanted anyone to know. I've never told anyone that, until you right now."

Quickly getting up from my chair, I walked over and put both my arms around her and said, "Grandma, I'm so sorry that happened to you. I'm so sorry you've had to carry that dark secret for so long. Can I pray for you?" I asked, as I sat down on the footstool in front of her chair.

"Yes, you can," she said softly.

As we prayed together, I felt a closeness to Grandma that I hadn't experienced since I was a boy. When we finished praying, she suddenly stood up from her rocking chair and said, "I'll be right back in just a minute; I have something I want to give you." She left the room and was gone for about ten minutes.

When she returned, she handed to me an old black book tied together with a black cord; I'd never seen it before. It had a picture of a man and a beautiful woman sitting at a table that she had sketched and taped on the front, with the simple title, *Poems*.

"This is a little book of poems I put together when I was just a girl," she said with a bashful, vulnerable look I'd never seen on her face before. "Aw, thank you, Grandma! I can't believe that you've never showed me this before!"

"Well, I haven't showed it to anyone in many years," she said with a nervous giggle.

As I opened the book to read a few of the poems inside, I noticed she had written on the inside cover, "1943"—the year she was seventeen. The pages were very delicate, yellowed, and weathered by time, so I carefully turned each one. The common thread in every poem was heartache, disappointment, and loneliness.

The combination of the story Grandma had told just me about her uncle, and the gloomy words expressed in her poems, provided a clearer picture behind the fear, shame, and constant worry I'd recognized in her all my life.

"Thank you, Grandma. I love it," I said gratefully, knowing I'd just been given a rare treasure. It was a piece of my fragile grandmother's heart that she had allowed few others to see.

> *It's just a poor heart lonely and blue*
> *It's just a poor heart thinking of you*
> *Darling please come back or you'll break it in two*
> *It's just a poor heart waiting for you*

> *Jean Dehaven, 1943*

CHAPTER 16

——— ༉ ———

AFTER I RETURNED home from Grandma Fannie's funeral, I started volunteering at the church periodically and became involved with the intercessory prayer ministry. The second time I attended one of the Sunday-morning prayer meetings, I noticed the same sharply dressed, high-heeled, black-haired woman I'd seen before. With noticeable confidence and a businesslike persona, she approached me purposely after the meeting and introduced herself.

"Hi, I'm Sofia," she said with a warm smile and firm handshake. "I'm the Director of Intercessory Prayer."

"Hi, Sofia, I'm Shawn," I responded somewhat shyly.

"I remember seeing you here last Sunday morning, but I didn't get a chance to meet you," she added. "How long have you been coming to church here?"

The more I opened up to her, the more questions she asked, and with her disarming disposition, I felt completely comfortable answering each one.

In just a short time, Sofia and I became good friends and our unlikely friendship strengthened all the more after she hired me as her personal trainer. It was hard for me to understand why someone like Sofia wanted anything to do with me, but she seemed to see something in me that I didn't see in myself. It was as though God had strategically brought her into my life for a purpose and somehow, she knew it.

I could barely even lift my eyes when I walked into the church, so heavy was the shame I continued to carry. But my burdened head seemed to rise a little higher each time I had the opportunity to spend time with my new nurturing friend. A young widow, Sofia was about the same age as my ex-wife Andrea and she knew about suffering in pain and hardship.

My respect and admiration for Sofia deepened as she shared with me the details of her husband's tragic death following a sudden heart attack while he was working out with his trainer at a large commercial gym. Her story and her willingness to open up to me about something so traumatic moved me.

Before his death just two years before, Sofia's husband had been a successful broker for many professional athletes in Houston. This enabled him to provide his wife and two children a very privileged lifestyle. Unfortunately, his premature death left too many pots on the fire, forcing Sofia to use much of her inheritance to tie up all her husband's loose ends and put her kids through school.

Although she still lived comfortably, the pampered lifestyle Sofia and her children had grown accustomed to—living in a grand home with a full-time housekeeper, cook, and gardener—was gone. She refused to be resentful, though, and being a smart businesswoman in her own right, Sofia took the reins with both hands, guided the circumstances life had given her, and plowed forward. I often thought that even with all she'd accomplished, the most impressive thing about her was her unusual ability to maintain a grateful heart.

When Sofia saw me struggling to find new personal-training clients in the suburbs, she came up with the idea for me to start a fitness class at the church. In just a short time, through her close connections with church leadership, I began teaching a circuit-training class two evenings a week. I was completely floored when Sofia insisted on purchasing all of the exercise equipment for me.

I learned very quickly that once Sofia set her mind to do something, it was really difficult to move her away from it. However, she possessed such a rare ability to maneuver through it with such grace and humility that I felt as though I were the one helping *her.*

Being a fitness professional surprisingly turned out to be an unexpected door opener for me, and I eventually had the opportunity to train and become friends with several of the pastors and their wives. Unfortunately for me, few suburbanites had the desire and the discipline to maintain their fitness regimen with the same commitment as my clients in the city.

Over the months, we continued to become closer friends and as Sofia heard more of my life story, she encouraged me to engage in a deep, emotional healing prayer method.

Sofia and her friend Maryjane had both been trained and certified in this particular method, which was becoming very popular in churches all across the nation. According to Sofia, this intimate prayer method involved helping the participant gain a greater awareness around the true source of deep emotional pain, and inviting God's healing into the earliest memory connected to it. Desperate for answers and highly intrigued about this new method, I decided to take her up on it and met with the two of them in a private room at the church two weeks later.

Feeling anxious and a little nervous when I first arrived, I sat down in the chair facing Sofia and Maryjane as they comforted me with their caring smiles.

I had no idea what to expect or what intimate details they might ask about my life, but I'd already settled in my mind that I would try my best to be completely honest about it all. They spent the better part of an hour asking me all sorts of questions about my life before we transitioned into prayer.

"Shawn, it's very evident by our discussion that you're carrying deep feelings of *helplessness* and *not being enough*," Maryjane said. "I want you to close your eyes and think about the earliest memory you can remember feeling helpless. Once you're able locate the memory, please just nod your head," she added.

Within seconds, I nodded my head as the memory of the night my father threatened to kill my mother on a dark country road filled my mind. I felt the fear and anxiety resurrect from deep inside myself as I visualized the car parked on the side of road with me locked inside, frantically banging on the widow, trying to get out to help my mother.

"Okay, Shawn," Maryjane interjected with a loving tone. "Describe to us what you see."

As I related this painful memory in vivid detail, Maryjane continued, "Now, Shawn, I want you visualize Jesus opening the car door to help you and climbing into the back seat with you. Can you see that?"

"Yes, I can see it," I said in a somber tone.

"Now I want you to listen, and allow Him to speak to you in that car," she said warmly.

After a few moments went by, she asked, "What is He saying to you, Shawn?"

"He's saying that He's with me, and that I'm not alone," I responded.

"God is always with you, Shawn," Sofia said softly, "and if He's with you, you're never helpless, are you?"

"No," I responded with a smile as my eyes filled with tears.

After this, we continued for another 45 minutes or so, applying the same process to several other specific memories centered on my mother, my stepfather, and his family.

When we finished and were collecting our belongings, Sophia turned to me and said, "Shawn, there are obviously so many layers to all of this pain in your life. It's going to take some time to unravel all of it. I know this is really hard for you, but I want to encourage you to consider doing more of these prayer sessions with us."

"Okay," I said thoughtfully. "I don't have any problem with that. When would you like to meet again?" They both smiled as we scheduled to meet the following Tuesday afternoon.

As the three of us walked out of the room together into the long hallway which led to one of the glass entryways of the megachurch, Sofia put her arm around Maryjane and said light heartedly, "Well, Maryjane, it looks like we've finally discovered our own Sybil to work with (referring to the Oscar-winning film about the abused girl with multiple personalities)."

"Thanks a lot!" I said in a playful tone. "I'm glad to be of service."

We all laughed as we got into our cars and went our separate ways.

I saw Sofia the following morning during her training session with me at the gym in Houston. When we finished, I walked her out to her car so we could chat for a while, since my next client had canceled.

"Shawn! That prayer session yesterday was so powerful, wasn't it?" she said somewhat dramatically.

"Yes, it was really intense," I responded.

"Maryjane and I were discussing it last night on the phone," she said. "I think it's more than a coincidence that we both individually had the same perception, which we believe is a pivotal piece to your emotional healing."

"Really?" I asked with heightened interest. "What was that?"

"First of all," she said compassionately as she put her hand on my shoulder, "I want to say how heartbroken we both were to hear about all you went through as a child. No child should ever have to suffer like that!"

"Thank you for saying that, Sofia; it really means a lot."

Leaning in, Sophia softly said, "The part I was referring to that Maryjane and I both recognized has to do with the way you minimize the part your mother played in your abuse. Do you see how you do that?" After a moment of silence she added, "I really don't think you do."

"Shawn," she said with heightened passion, "most mothers would have taken you and run! You talked so much about feeling the need to protect your mother from your father and stepfather, but who was there to protect *you*?!"

Trying desperately to process her words and stay present, I mumbled out the words with a blank stare, "No one."

Once again softening her voice as she obviously noticed my distress, she said, "Shawn, you were just a child, sweetheart, and it wasn't your job to protect her. *You* needed to be protected *from* her. I'm sorry, dear friend, if it hurts you to hear this," she continued, "but as far as Maryjane and I are concerned, we believe your mother was your worst abuser of all. You went to her again and again and told her what was happening, but she refused to listen. She had the power make it stop and she chose not to. I find what she did to be completely criminal!"

I'm sure the blank look of confusion forming on my face said it all. "It is a lot to wrap my head around," I responded, dazed at all I'd just heard.

"I'm sure it is," Sophia said with genuine compassion. "You've worked through a lot of things in your life, Shawn, but realistically, I don't think you've even begun to uncover the deepest root of your pain: your mother."

I was having such a difficult time, *not* because what I hearing was contrary to what I'd told others all my adult life (and it was), but because my heart was confirming that it was true and my fragile mind was screaming *not* to go there!

The part that began to bother me more and more in the days ahead was the troubling question that rolled around in my head: "If my mind has been protecting me from the truth by rearranging my relationship with my mother, what else has it hidden from me?"

My life had changed so dramatically in such a short time that people around me began to notice. Many of the gay people in the Houston gym I'd known for years before my "come back to Jesus days" were having a difficult time understanding my new transformation from gay one day to straight the next.

Most of them seemed confused about it and some were even offended. Even though I only opened up to my closest friends about my personal life, others speculated. Whenever anyone approached me wanting details, I emphasized that my intentions had nothing to do with the judgment of others, and that I was doing only what I felt necessary for myself.

However, the tension continued to rise for me when Darius, a six-foot-five trainer with a shaved head and tattoos, decided the best way he could support his gay friends from feeling judged was to bully me in front of them. Even as a grown man in my thirties, my big biceps proved no match for the monstrous fear that bullying still brought up for me.

Eventually, I limited my training in the Houston gym to three days a week, after I conveniently discovered that the congested freeways (which caused me to take as long as an hour and a half to get home) provided the perfect buffer (excuse) between my newest bully and me—a mental diversion technique I'd spent many years refining.

Around this time, I also began leading a weekly Bible study at the gym. The gym's owner Leo, who'd recently started attending church with me, offered up his private office every Wednesday morning for the few of us who regularly attended. As we continued to meet together, it didn't take long before Leo and I, along with another trainer named Ethan, became good friends. Leo and Ethan had both been involved in competitive body building and had lots more experience than I did in the fitness industry. I took full advantage of the opportunity to learn more from them and really enjoyed working out with them as often as I could.

The strenuous weight training and fitness goals we set became a great deterrent for me against drinking and drugging, enabling me to stay sober for longer stretches of time. As our friendship continued to develop, I eventually opened up to Leo and Ethan about my drug use and HIV status.

I actually found the warm response and encouragement from my masculine new friends a strangely unexpected source of healing. It felt strange that the God of the Universe would choose a smelly gym as an emotional healing center for me, and unexpected because no matter how hard I tried, I obviously still didn't have this God thing all figured out.

As the weeks went by, the times I drove in to the Houston gym and then took the long drive back to the suburbs felt like punishment. I returned on those days to my single chair by the window. I had a beautiful view, but loneliness was the only one I had to share it with. After months of living in such isolated conditions, I sometimes felt that I would absolutely lose my mind.

One afternoon, my sanity was suddenly rescued when Leo and I realized that the beach house his family owned was just five minutes from
my new apartment. He said that he and his wife Victoria would occasionally take their two kids there for the weekend. Eventually, they
started inviting me to dinner with them and to hang out at the beach
house when they were there.

Before long, these occasions became more frequent and I absolutely
fell in love with Leo and Victoria's two adorable kids, Madison and
Patrick. Victoria, also in the fitness industry, wasn't into the church
thing at all, but we soon developed a sibling-like connection nonetheless. She often affectionately referred to me as her little brother.

Victoria and I shared an interest in fashion and home décor and
would often sit looking at magazines together while the kids played
and Leo tinkered with some project. On several occasions while we
were alone, Victoria said to me, "Shawn, I think you're an absolutely
beautiful person just as you are, and I hope that one day you'll fully
realize that. As a mother, I would be completely thrilled to have a
son just like you!"

Of course, I knew what she was referring to, and although I tried not
to think about it too much, there were times I couldn't deny how the
power of her encouraging words lifted my heart. Once again, I could
see God using an unexpected source in an unconventional way to
minister life to me.

When I first moved into my new apartment in Galveston County, I got
rid of my TV in order to open up more time for prayer, Bible study, and
journaling. Although I'd also spent time engaging in these spiritual
disciplines while I living with the Bianchis in Mississippi, I now spent
nearly as much time on these pursuits as I had as a young pastor.

I spent a lot of time reading Christian books on theology, church history, emotional and physical healing, breaking strongholds, and current books by well-known Christian authors. I also listened to countless teaching CDs and daily played a CD from a popular preacher reciting scriptures on healing.

I felt a sense of closeness to God that I hadn't felt since my days of full-time ministry, but my thinking was definitely shifting. The experiences I had in the prayer sessions with Sofia and Maryjane had opened my eyes in an unusual way. They led me to start looking for answers in a way I never had before. When I was younger, I took in everything my mentors taught me, refusing to question any of it. Now, I gave myself permission to question everything, and I somehow found the courage to start facing my fears when it came to looking at things with a different perspective.

As I began to trudge through this new road of research with fresh eyes and openness, it became very apparent to me how many discrepancies and viewpoints there had been in all the various circles of Christianity throughout the years. Having a bachelor's degree in theology, I knew there were many varied streams of thought, but I had never seemed to recognize all the evidence which so clearly substantiates God's involvement in maintaining measures of mystery as I did this time.

I could easily see the recurring cycle throughout history that those who are the most dogmatic about *having God all figured out* are often the most susceptible to use their knowledge as means to capitalize on control, manipulation, and dominance.

In all of my of my studies, along with my own personal experiences and interactions with well-respected leaders in Christendom, I found one consistent factor which continuously gets in the way and messes things up: our humanness. Even when we seem to have all the best intentions and possess genuine, humble hearts, we still miss the mark. We do so because deep inside us all, there are personal opinions, experiences, prejudices, racism, sexism, bigotry, emotional hurts, and disowned parts of ourselves that we unconsciously try to conceal behind masks and respectable positions.

In this place of questioning and added awareness, I began to open my mind about the scriptures in a way I had been unwilling to do for my entire life. I still wholeheartedly believed the scriptures were inspired by God as a message of hope and redemption to all mankind, but I was also able to recognize and accept that they were written through impure vessels which are incapable of perfection.

A perfect example of how God can work through us so powerfully in certain areas even when we are unable to see clearly in others was on full display the day I went to Sofia's house for Thanksgiving dinner. As I pulled up in front of her beautiful new home that afternoon, I looked forward to another of her delicious home cooked meals. I'd been there a few times before and each time I arrived, I noticed another landscaping project she'd masterfully completed with beautiful detail.

Sofia had recently had the house built after she was forced to downsize from the monstrosity she and her husband and children had lived in. However, it was easy to see that she was still doing very well: her new home was in an exclusive gated subdivision and her next-door neighbor was a famous professional basketball star.

Sofia was a class act and I had no doubts that she would make the day really special for all her guests. However, I was not looking forward to spending more time around her very entitled, boisterous 23-year-old daughter Camila. Just a few months before, Camila had shamelessly flaunted herself at me during a few of my circuit-training classes, and I couldn't stand the way she talked down to her mother. When I entered the house, I was relieved to see that she had brought a new boyfriend. Although this distraction kept her away from me, it didn't seem to help in taming her tongue.

The biggest surprise of the day came from my interaction with Sofia's son Thomas, who was on break from medical school with his roommate Devin. I'd only met Thomas during a five-minute introduction following a church service one night when he had come home for the weekend. Even though it was very brief, I still had my suspicions—and my suspicion meter went completely off the scale as soon as Devin walked into the kitchen to meet me: He was most definitely gay, and so was Thomas.

I didn't just surmise this from Devin's mannerisms; I *knew* he was gay because he pursued me the entire day. It was so blatant and apparent at times that I was completely embarrassed by it.

The obvious questions that dominated my thoughts throughout the remainder of the day and the days that followed:

"Does Sofia realize that her son is gay?"

"Maybe she recognized it all along and that's what drew her to me? If so, is she somehow hoping that if I find healing from homosexuality, I can help her son?"

"But then again, why would she keep this from me, when we've opened up to each other about so many things?"

There was also the other possibility—the one all the signs told me was true: She just didn't see it.

"How ironic," I thought, *"that the very one God used to bring a reality check into my life about my relationship with my mother has her own eyes closed to a crucial truth about her son!"*

In this time when so much of my thinking was being challenged, there was also one other gnawing question I couldn't seem to escape from:

"If her son and I are both gay from God's design, what if God brought me into her life to help her accept it?"

It was a lot to take in, and with everything else that was beginning to unfold in my life, the stress and confusion of it all was clearly taking a toll on me. I'd been at the church for two years and I was still struggling in so many ways. Nothing had changed in me regarding same-sex attraction. If anything, my desire for a committed relationship with a man who shared my values only intensified.

Adding to my confusion, my friend Ethan became really clingy and jealous over my friendship with Leo. When I talked with Leo about it, he admitted thinking that Ethan had a crush on me. It was the last thing I wanted to hear, with all the other confusion and conflict in my life, so I just insensitively cut him off instead of dealing with it as a true friend should.

My financial pressures mounted as I continued struggling to maintain long-term training clients in the suburbs such as I had in the city. By the time I gave my ten-percent tithe to the church every month, there were times I didn't have enough money left to buy groceries. I'd done everything I'd been instructed by the church leadership to do, and even so, I was barely making it. I felt that I was about to go under and I wondered if it had all been my own doing.

It was also becoming very obvious that Sofia had developed feelings for me and hoped that one day we'd be together. Although I tried my best to never lead her on in any way, I was starting to feel pressure and discomfort in her presence. She had done so much to help me, and the last thing I wanted to do was hurt her.

I felt compelled to leave the church and move back into the city, but using her persuasive personality, Sofia encouraged me to hold on just a little longer. She told me that the senior associate pastor had asked her if she thought I was ready to return to ministry and she had told him I was. She said he'd responded, "I hope you're right, Sofia, because things are about to open up for him."

After all this time, the opportunity of returning to public ministry stared me directly in the face. I thought it had been lost to me forever. And honestly, a part of me didn't know if I even wanted it anymore. Again, I felt submerged in a sea of confusing questions.

I received all the answers I needed, though, and in the most painful way imaginable when I learned that Pastor Jeffrey and Kaela had shared my confidential information with others in the church, right down to my being gay and HIV positive. Horrified, crushed, betrayed, and shamed all over again, I left the church and those isolated suburbs.

A few months after I'd moved back to Houston, I ran into Jose, one of the young men I used to see singing on the worship team with Pastor Jeffrey. He came up to me when he saw me and said, "Shawn, I noticed you left the church a while back."

"Yeah, a few months ago," I responded.

"I guess I probably left right after you then," he admitted.

"You did?!" I asked. "Why?"

"Yeah," he continued, "one Friday night while I was hanging out at Jeffrey and Kaela's house drinking margaritas, Jeffrey tried to kiss me after Kaela went to bed. I was really close with Kaela and I didn't know how to deal with it, so I just left."

Suddenly, so many mysteries were solved: the odd conversations I had with them Jeffrey and Kaela; the way they rejected me after I wouldn't drink with them; the awkward way I often felt they were each attracted to me, but didn't want to accept; and the cruel way Kaela shamed me when I was still in the darkness of despair after I relapsed, telling me she was "glad it happened" because I was "becoming too self-righteous."

My memory returned to the time Jeffrey told me he was helping a young man, a sound technician he'd been mentoring, who was about to leave for college as he worked through his homosexuality. Jeffrey asked if he could pick my brain about helping this young gay man, and we spent several hours on the phone as Jeffrey gleaned information on where gay people like to go, how they recognize and signal each other, and many other aspects of gay life. Finding out that Jeffrey had tried to kiss Jose, I had to wonder whether this gay research had been for Jeffrey himself.

The hurt and betrayal I felt from both of my pastors went beyond words. I trusted them and they obviously used my personal pain to make themselves feel better.

I knew I could have sued the megachurch because of the HIPPA Law, (which protects those of us who have HIV from having our status shared), but I decided to let God deal with it. Strangely enough, I received a call from a senior pastor I knew from a church in Dallas not long after this revelation. He told me Jeffrey had applied for the worship-leader position at his church after he and Kaela resigned their positions in Houston. (The rumor was they were asked to resign because of betraying me, along with possible drug use.) The pastor wanted to know if I knew any details of their departure from the church and whether I would be willing to share them with him.

Although it wasn't my usual practice to tell all the dirt on someone, in light of everything that had occurred, I shared perhaps more than the inquiring pastor had anticipated.

CHAPTER 17

———— ⚹ ————

As I sat at my desk catching up on paperwork before the next patient came into the wellness center, I stared blindly at my computer, thinking about how dramatically my life had changed in such a short time. It seemed like overnight that I'd gone from not having enough work to having more work than I could handle—and I loved feeling productive again!

I was working part-time with patients who had life-threatening diseases—many with HIV, AIDS, cancer, and diabetes—at a wellness center affiliated with a community clinic. The rest of my time, I worked with my own personal-training clients at two other fitness facilities. The clinic in Houston that employed me was one of only a few in the country to have successfully transitioned from treating strictly LGBT patients during the AIDS epidemic in the 1980s to serving the general population.

My new social-service environment looked nothing like my circuit-training classes at the megachurch in South Houston. There was no one wearing designer fitness attire, and no one trying to prevent her big diamond rings from cutting into her fingers while she did her bicep curls. Instead, there was Felicia, a Latina transgender woman who walked around the facility three days a week flaunting her figure and flipping her long hair; a few heterosexual women; and lots of gay men. Some of the patients were muscular, some overweight, and others emaciated by the dreadful diseases trying to take their lives.

At first, I was quite nervous and tense, feeling out of place in this new environment. Several of the patients I worked with also struggled with mental illness, which had always been uncomfortable for me to be around. But after a few short months, I fell in love with this courageous mishmash of souls. I could see the tremendous amount of resilience required for them to keep coming back week after week, some taking two hours of public transportation each way to make their appointments, and I wanted to do all I could to help them.

One of my responsibilities was training patients for a two-year heart study which was being conducted by a well-respected college of medicine located in the Houston Medical Center, and administered through our clinic. This extensive trial focused on adults with HIV and elevated triglycerides; we put them through a twenty-four-week lifestyle modification of diet, exercise, and medication. The data collected from this research was significant for the long-term care of those living with HIV and AIDS.

Working at the clinic returned to me a sense of purpose that I'd not felt since my days in full-time ministry. It also forced me to start dealing with the denial I'd been living in for several years about my own health, and the sobering fact I had HIV.

The reality of it all hit me so hard that I must have cried myself to sleep just about every night the first month I worked at the clinic. I cried for the twenty-three year old kid who'd just found out he was HIV positive; for the gentle woman taking chemo who refused to give up; for the guy with a "buffalo hump" on his back (from years of taking old-school HIV meds), who was now covered head to toe with red, swollen hives; and for the patients who obviously didn't have very long to live. I probably cried more for myself.

"What if I end up like one of these patients?" At first, I couldn't seem to get that terrifying thought out of my head, but as I continued to show up and care for these brave people, my fears took a back seat to meeting the needs of the precious hearts in front of me.

Five years had passed since my HIV diagnosis, and I had dragged my feet as long as I possibly could. With the chronic fatigue I was experiencing on a regular basis and my increasing viral load, my doctor urged me to start taking medication. Much of my apprehension about beginning an HIV medication regimen came from my own history of hypersensitivity to medication (which probably did me more harm than good psychologically). I had often experienced adverse reactions when I took just about any kind of medication, and the possible HIV medication side effects I'd read about terrified me.

My nightmare turned into reality the day I started putting the five highly toxic horse-sized pills into my body. I had reactions that my doctor said he'd never seen before: I had diarrhea for the first two weeks and my stomach felt upside down most of the time; I broke out with bad acne and lost lots of hair; I had annoying hot flashes and would break out in sweats with no warning. Worst of all, I had a very difficult time concentrating, problem solving, and short-term memory loss, which made it almost impossible some days to get any work done.

My doctor encouraged me to hang on, promising me that things would get better; but after two months of struggling, I honestly didn't know how much longer I could do it. Fortunately, I was working at a clinic where people understood. My caring supervisor was very understanding and supportive. It was as though God knew all along where I needed to be to make this difficult transition, and after another month, my side effects subsided.

During this time, I met Elliot, an overweight, fifty-year-old gay man with curly hair and a huge, charismatic personality. Elliot was CFO and Acting Director of the clinic, and he eventually hired me as his personal trainer. When I first began working with Elliot, I trained him two evenings a week at the wellness center (a separate location from the main clinic) after hours when it was closed to patients. From the beginning, he made it very clear that he wanted only to exercise and had no desire to change his unhealthy diet.

Elliot was very high strung and suffered from chronic back pain just as I did. Because I personally had lots of experience with both, I knew exactly how to work with him. He was also used to being in charge, so I tried my best to never make him feel as if I were talking down to him or telling him what to do. I'd learned over the years that the best way to train successful leaders is to stay conscientious of how challenging it can be for them to hand over their control to another person, especially to one who might be perceived as only a "gym rat".

After a few months of training, Elliot began to experience some relief from his back pain and slowly started to allow me to help him change his toxic diet. Over time, he increased his training with me to three mornings a week, lost three pants sizes, and had to buy a whole new wardrobe. He was hooked!

Elliot had made exercise and healthy eating a way of life, and he never stopped telling me how much better his life was because of it. Helping people change their lives as Elliot did continued to be the most rewarding part of my job, and made the long hours I put in worthwhile.

During the months I was coaching Elliot into a healthier way of living, he took upon himself the job of coaching me out from under my mound of HIV shame. When we first started working together, the wellness center was completely empty in the evenings, providing us complete privacy to dig deeply into conversation.

Elliot was a gifted conversationalist, although he struggled with boundaries. I sometimes found his questioning quite intrusive and inappropriate, but the conversations we dived into presented me a seemingly safe way to process through so many unanswered questions, such as: *"Are my best years behind me now that I have HIV? How do I tell others I'm HIV positive? Does having HIV limit me to only dating others with HIV?"* And the hardest one of all for me: *"Do I really want to come out again and stay out for good?"*

In some of our discussions, Elliot also opened up to me and shared that he still struggled with survivor's guilt from watching so many of his close friends, including his own life-partner, die from AIDS. He said that helping me helped him continue to work through some of his own pain. He even gave me a ceramic angel Christmas ornament, which had belonged to his best friend who'd died of AIDS years before, as a Christmas gift (even though Elliot was Jewish). He said that his friend had blonde hair like me, as well as other similarities, and he hoped he would be able to help me in ways that he hadn't been able to help his friend. I felt very humbled and honored by his desire to help me, although a small part of me could see that he might be adopting me unconsciously as a substitute to work through some of his own unfinished business.

As Elliot and I continued to confide in each other, we developed an undeniably strong friendship; however, as with most people who struggle with boundaries, we also developed an equally strong co-dependency.

Elliot encouraged me to use my leadership background to bring some positive changes to the wellness center. Happy for the opportunity and with the full support of my supervisor Connie, I began tackling some of the old ways of doing things that were benefiting only a few people instead of everyone. I also started a monthly healthy-living seminar for patients and staff as a source of motivation.

Overall, most of the patients and staff coming into the facility were enjoying the changes and the more uplifting environment, but there was a small, pessimistic clique (which had basically had the run of the place for several years) that didn't want change and began to cause problems. Brenton, the chief antagonist of this group, who had at one time served on the board of directors for the organization, started challenging us at every turn.

With an unwarranted sense of entitlement, Brenton went as far making phone calls to members of the board, trying to get my supervisor Connie fired.

The tense atmosphere that began to permeate the wellness center whenever he and his gossipy clique came around made it very difficult for me to come to work some days. However, Brenton's shenanigans eventually backfired when Elliot got wind of what was going on. With one quick phone call, Elliot ended the reign of King Brenton, making sure he was never allowed back into the wellness center. Probably in a state of shock that their leader had been ousted, his tightly knit band of comrades stayed away for a few days, and we all enjoyed some peace as a result.

Unfortunately, the peace was short lived when just a few days later, I received a call from my supervisor Connie informing me that Cletus, one of the other guys from the same bunch had emailed her, making physical threats towards me. She said that she would leave it up to me as to whether I would report to work, permitting me to take the day off until they investigated the matter further. She said that if I did decide to come in, they wanted me to park in front of the building and be escorted in from my car, just to be safe. Backing down from the situation was the last thing I thought I should do, so I opted for the escort. Even though I knew Cletus struggled with mental illness and the whole thing would probably blow over quickly, it didn't seem to help much with the increasing anxiety I felt.

While all this was going on, a patient I was taking through our six-week training program began to sexually harass me. When he wasn't asking me out or finding ways to put his hands on me (in an eerie way that caught me by surprise each time), he would blatantly look me up and down as if he wanted to devour me. It was easy to see by the look on his face that he realized he was making me feel uncomfortable, and he seemed to enjoy it. There was also something else about him that troubled me: I felt a heightened anxiety each time he had a particular tattoo on his arm exposed. Although I was aware that it frightened me, I couldn't seem to wrap my head around why it did.

A few weeks before this patient's program ended, he also started writing me letters, but I threw them away or gave them to the other trainer I worked with just to get rid of them. Although I know now, I should have ended his training program and reported him; at the time, I didn't feel that I had the option. I really didn't even see how much of a predator he was, nor did I realize the extent of my emotional triggering by him; I knew only that I felt extremely uncomfortable in his presence and I wanted out. I felt that I was supposed to just suck it up and get through it: my pattern of response in situations such as this.

For several nights, I couldn't sleep from worrying; full of fear and anxiety, unable to stop the wheel of obsessive thoughts spinning in my head. By the third night, I was absolutely exhausted, and must have tossed and turned in my bed a hundred times before I eventually saw the morning sun peeking through my tightly drawn drapes. When I eventually climbed out of bed, I felt a wave of anxiety hit me full force in a way that terrified me. Something was definitely wrong.

When I walked out to my kitchen, I sensed that someone was watching me. I could feel the eyes following my every move; but how could the person see me? I started looking everywhere: behind the big chair in the corner, inside the kitchen cabinets, in the closets, on the balcony outside my large window. *"Where is he hiding?!"*

I surmised that my apartment was bugged and had hidden cameras. After I looked around, I was sure that there was a camera in the AC vent. I pulled a barstool over to the wall where the vent was and climbed up trying to reach it, but it was still too high for me to see inside.

As I climbed back down and jumped off of the barstool, another wave of paranoia hit me; I was quickly shifting into full panic mode.

I grabbed my cell phone to call my friends Allie and Joan, a same-sex couple I'd recently reconnected with. When no one answered, I left them a hysterical message, telling them someone was watching me through hidden cameras in my apartment; I was sure the person wanted to hurt me. I begged them to please call me back because I didn't know what to do.

After I hung up, I ran to the door because I sensed that someone was outside my door waiting to break in. I looked through the peephole over and over until I felt like my heart was going to break through my chest from the immense pressure of anxiety. Finally, unable to take it anymore, I unlocked the door and flung it open. No one was there!

After a few seconds, I worked up the courage to step up to the door and stick my head out. I felt a small sense of relief after I looked down the hallway in front of my apartment in both directions and found no one there. I decided if someone were going to come and get me, I wanted to be able to see the person coming, so I left my door wide open. I was looking for a legal pad and a pen when Allie called me back. After she talked with me for a few minutes and realized the fragile state I was in, she asked me to not leave, assuring me that she and Joan would be right over. Before I hung up, I asked her to please bring a gun with her so she could protect us when they got here.

While I was waiting, I found the legal pad I'd been looking for, sat down on a bar stool in front the kitchen island facing the open door to my apartment, and I began writing obsessively. I wrote page after page, as though my very survival depended on it. Occasionally, I would pause from the process, start sobbing uncontrollably while begging God to help me, and then return to my writing frenzy.

At first, I wrote about not feeling wanted and accepted by my family, but after breaking into sobs a few times, my mind shifted and I started to create—just as I had when I was alone in my room as a child. I began creating a business plan. I wrote until my hand was completely numb and physically refused to participate any longer.

Allie and Joan walked in. Seeing my heightened distress and hearing that I hadn't slept much in three days, they urged me to go into my bedroom and lie down. Joan sat beside me talking softly, trying to calm me.

About thirty minutes later, Allie came into my bedroom with her cell phone and said, "Shawn, Elliot's on the phone and wants to talk to you."

After I spoke with him for a few minutes, Elliot said, "Shawn, there is someone here I would like you to speak with."

Quickly realizing that the woman on the other end of the phone was trying to psychoanalyze me, I started feeling defensive, trying to out-smart her questioning.

It didn't seem very long after I ended the call that Elliot arrived at my apartment. At some point, he must have also contacted Sofia because of the close friendship he knew I had with her and explained to her the condition I was in, because she arrived shortly after he did. The four of them—Allie, Joan, Elliot, and Sofia—eventually drove me to the hospital, where I was taken into a small room for examination. Since Joan was nine months pregnant at the time, Elliot told her and Allie to go home and get some rest.

Elliot and Sofia stayed with me in the little room during the examination process. I remember answering each question the nurse asked me obsessively, as though I couldn't stop myself from talking; feeling the dire need to cover every little detail. I also remember feeling very puffed up and self-righteous, as though I were someone of great importance.

From there, the three of us were transported in a van to a different facility. I remember feeling surprised that it was dark outside; the episode had lasted the entire day. While we were in transport, my hallucinations increased. By the time the van pulled up in front of the double glass doors, I saw myself stepping out in front of a cheering crowd, lavishly expressing love and support for me. But when Elliot, who was standing beside me, handed my arm over to the attendant who stepped out from behind one of the glass doors, the cheering stopped abruptly.

The attendant led me through the glass doors and into a waiting room, where he gave me a clipboard with several pages of paperwork to read through and sign. My anxiety and fear rose to new heights when I realized *I couldn't see the words!* The only option I felt I had was to ask where to sign, and I did. They asked me if I understood what I'd just read each time before I signed, but I was too terrified to tell them I couldn't.

All I could think was, *"Why would Elliot do this to me? Doesn't he know—I'll die in here!"*

CHAPTER 18

⎯⎯⎯⎯ ♇ ⎯⎯⎯⎯

Two months later, while Elliot and I were having lunch, he caught my eye. Leaning in with a kind, compassionate expression, he asked, "Shawn, do realize what happened to you?"

I paused for a moment and then soberly responded, "Yeah--I know. It's still a lot to wrap my head around sometimes, but I'm aware."

I didn't know for sure when my awareness had come, but I could definitely tell things had shifted. For a while after I left the hospital, things were still pretty chaotic: I talked as though I had no control to stop; I couldn't drive to the store or find my way home without calling someone to help me with directions. When I did venture out, I would panic from being around too many people, and would have to leave suddenly. My mind was still so fragile that I had to have Sofia come over to my apartment a few times and help me pay my bills. For weeks after my release from the hospital, I worked so obsessively rearranging and redecorating my apartment that I had to set a timer to remind me when to stop and take a break to eat.

"Do you remember when Sofia and I came to visit you the following evening, after we took you to hospital?" Elliot asked.

"Yeah, I remember parts of it," I responded.

"It wasn't until then that we both realized how much you suffered as a child," Elliot admitted. "Memory after memory came pouring out of you, and some of it was really hard for both of us to listen to, but we knew you needed to let it out. You pleaded with Sofia and me to get you out of there, but we were afraid for you to leave prematurely. It seemed as though some of the things you were experiencing in there were triggering hidden memories for you, and we didn't want to interfere with the process; like the two guys with long hair you saw in there with Ohio accents and tattoos you said frightened you. That's why I told you if you still wanted to check out, and could gain enough composure to call me, I would come and get you."

Then, shaking his head, Elliot said, "I was completely surprised when you called me two days later. I thought it was still too soon, but I wanted to keep my promise."

"I can't imagine how confusing all of this has been for you," I told Elliot. "I so appreciate all you've done for me! It's scary to think what would've happened to me if you hadn't been there to walk me through all this. But I have to beg of you," I added with a serious tone, "please don't ever put me in a place like that again! I don't know if I could survive a second time."

Touching my arm, Elliot kindly responded, "Shawn, I'm so sorry for taking you there, but based on the little information I knew at the time, I really didn't know what else to do."

"Thank you for saying that, and I completely understand why you did," I assured him.

The whole ordeal had been the darkest of nightmares, and it didn't end after I left the hospital. I had spent three terrifying days in the psych ward, where an attendant had mistreated me. He tried to put me in an isolated room with only a mat on the floor, and after I refused to go, he eventually over-medicated me so much that I almost knocked myself unconscious on the cement floor of the bathroom.

Shortly after I left the hospital, I'd also been diagnosed as bipolar, along with having chronic post-traumatic stress disorder, by a psychiatrist who worked for the same clinic that I did. The side effects I experienced when I first started taking my HIV medication were mild compared to the mind-altering drugs this doctor prescribed for me.

From the first time I met with this psychiatrist, I didn't trust him. I found him arrogant and condescending. It also infuriated me that he flirted with me during one of my private sessions, which made me trust him even less. I'm sure he probably thought I wouldn't mind, given the condition I was in. When I shared this with Elliot, he agreed to attend my next session with me. My psychiatrist was not happy.

About six weeks later, I discussed with my long-time primary-care physician—a personal friend who knew me well—everything that had been going on. He said, "Shawn, I'm very concerned about all of this. I can recognize the PTSD, but I have been treating you for a long time and have never thought you to be bipolar. I don't think you should be on these medications, and it troubles me to see what they are doing to you."

Somewhat hesitantly, he continued, "I probably shouldn't tell you this, but I have had some interactions with this same psychiatrist that you're seeing, and I agree with you: Something seems to be off with him. Now, you're fully aware that I'm not a psychiatrist, so I encourage you to get a second opinion, or even better, find a good psychotherapist and see what that person has to say."

Following my doctor's advice, I ditched my flirtatious psychiatrist and made an appointment to see a psychotherapist. To pay for the therapy, Elliot helped me secure a grant he knew was available to me because of my HIV status. How ironic that the HIV I thought was there to destroy me opened the door to the source that saved me.

It was as though God himself had hand-picked Ellie for me. With her short gray hair and sweet grandmotherly persona, I felt completely safe with her from the moment we met, and even more so after I learned she was a Christian. A semi-retired therapist with thirty years of experience at a highly respected teaching hospital in the Houston Medical Center, Ellie specialized in treating adults who had been sexually abused and traumatized as children. I met with her weekly at an LGBT counseling center in Montrose.

Fortunately, Ellie took only a short time to assure me that what my primary care doctor had suspected was accurate: I'd been misdiagnosed, and was *not* bipolar. She did agree that I had post-traumatic stress disorder, but she said she believed it would continue to subside as we worked together.

Ellie taught me that the brain is fully equipped to maneuver around occasional spikes of fear and trauma, quickly returning to its original baseline of serenity; however, the brain chemistry of an adult who was severally traumatized as a child is different. According to her, the baseline chemistry in the brain that tells the child he is safe and secure is completely altered; the greater the trauma, the higher the baseline is reset. She said for people like me who experienced long periods of trauma, rarely feeling safe, the baseline is set at a much higher level. Therefore, the brain moves into *flight or fight* rather quickly.

When I told Ellie how fearful I was of having another breakdown, she comforted me with the research that proved I could learn how to recognize when I was shifting into a heightened place of anxiety and could adopt self-calming techniques to bring myself back to my baseline of serenity. She assured me that if I did this, I wouldn't have to worry about future episodes of PTSD.

Ellie also said she believed my breakdown had everything to do with my mind finally reaching a tipping point. She said it was actually a common phenomenon for trauma survivors to have inexplicable breakdowns or occasional highly emotional episodes prior to treatment, as though the mind could only hold a certain amount of trauma before some pressure had to be released.

I actually found Ellie's words a source of great comfort because of the hidden fear I'd carried for so long over my fourth-grade breakdown, when my uncle found me shaking in my underwear, hiding in the bathtub like a frightened animal; and again, in my freshman year of college, when I was taken to the hospital by ambulance after having a seizure two weeks after my best friend had shunned me for unloading some of my childhood horror on him. The doctor who treated me in the university hospital had said he couldn't find anything medically wrong with me, and that the cause of my seizure was probably psychological. He referred me to a psychiatrist, but I never went.

I was relieved even further when Ellie told me what a miracle it was that I showed no signs of mental illness or personality disorders, which are often present in people with a history of severe childhood trauma. Because of the deep-seated fear I'd carried for so long about mental illness, which was so prevalent in my dad's family, it took Ellie many times to patiently reassure me that I didn't share this before I finally accepted it.

Over the course of the three years that I met weekly with Ellie, my world changed, as she continued to acknowledge the severity of the abuse I'd suffered as a child. She, just like Sofia and Maryjane, believed that my mother had been one of my abusers and a clear source of my inner torment.

Choosing to believe that my mom and I were both victims just trying to survive the big, bad wolves somehow helped me steady my mind from the trauma of the truth when I was a boy. If I had admitted to myself that my mom was just as guilty and responsible for all the pain I endured, then I had to accept that *everyone* I trusted to keep me safe when I was a child had, at one time or another, hurt me—even my precious grandmother. That's a hard reality for anyone to accept, and much more for a scared, unwanted child.

Ellie said that contrary to what many women who are domestically abused think, when a child witnesses such violence, there is no separation from the damage inflicted. Therefore, what I had seen done to my mother at the hands of first my father and later my stepfather when I was just a boy, I perceived to have also been done to me. There is no separation in the mind of a child.

Like most trauma survivors, my mind compartmentalized the pieces of my life as a coping mechanism. Many of the most painful pieces were hidden away and shoved back into a dark corner so I couldn't see them.

I'd developed such mastery at hiding characteristics about myself—traumatized, abused, gay, addicted, HIV positive—that my entire survival had been built around concealment since early childhood. The most damaging part: I was also hiding from myself.

Ellie said there were probably compartments in my mind that wouldn't be opened until sometime in the future, and some might never be opened. For the time being, she wanted me to focus on accessing the compartments that my mind was ready and willing to open. She explained that the more I was able to accept and integrate the disowned pieces of myself into my life, the healthier I would become.

This concept of compartmentalization also helped me understand and become much more compassionate toward my family members who were unable to acknowledge much of the pain and abuse in my life as well as their own. That's how their minds have coped and survived as well. My mom used to tell me that she couldn't remember anything before the age of eleven, which is a sign of trauma. My sister Hailey told me that Mom told her she had been raped by her stepbrother when she was a teenager; if she could remember that horror, there's no telling what her mind blocked out from her pre-teen years. The last time I went home to Ohio to visit, my grandmother shared with me that she had been molested by her uncle when she was a girl. She said that she was so ashamed by what happened that she never told anyone her entire life until she revealed it to me. It was easy to see how the cycle of pain and abuse often continues to from one generation to the next.

Each new piece of truth Ellie helped me uncover proved monumental for me because of the way I had always ruthlessly judged and criticized myself for never being enough. I began to see that so much I had always believed about myself and my family was untrue.

One of the most eye-opening sessions I had with Ellie occurred the day she told me that both my dad and my stepdad were psychopathic, and the trauma I suffered as a child equated to that of a holocaust survivor. I suddenly had the awareness of just how much I had mini-mized everything I endured as a child, just to survive, and also why I felt so drawn to movies and books that chronicled the lives of the tor-mented souls of the World War II era; I identified with them.

Although I minimized what I was going through when I was awake, my mind couldn't escape reality when I was asleep; that's why I had recur-ring nightmares of monsters and sinister characters trying to hurt me.

Learning more about myself helped; however, the harsh reality of it all proved hard to fathom at times. Each new compartment I opened often required a period of grieving. Ellie taught me the importance of acknowledging my feelings, and of giving myself permission to sit with them, instead of trying to change them just so I'd feel better. She taught me how to process my feelings and the necessity of giving my-self the opportunity to ask myself why and where they were coming from.

From Ellie, I also learned how to connect with Little Shawn, my in-ner child. She taught me the importance of visualizing myself as a strong, capable adult walking Little Shawn out of his darkness. She said I would need to parent Little Shawn and teach him all the things he never learned from his caretakers. It was now my responsibility to keep him safe. When he felt sad and needed to grieve, I needed to acknowledge that and give him the space to do it.

I was thinking about what Ellie had said to me about walking Little Shawn out of his darkness when I recalled a recurring dream I had dur-ing the time I was going to the church in south Houston.

I was walking through a very dark and gloomy forest, full of thorns, swamps, and deadly predators. At first it appeared as though the dream would not be any different from so many others I'd had through-out my life, having to fight and escape from those who were trying to harm me, until I saw him: the little blond boy, walking beside me with his hand in mine. He had shiny blond hair and features like mine, and I could feel that he was very special to me.

Suddenly, I turned around to see a viper about to strike him. I quickly lifted him up and swung him around out of reach just before the snake's fangs dug into his flesh. I ran with the boy in my arms and leaped over to the other side of a thick, swampy pool for safety. After I set the little boy down and comforted him, we continued hand-in-hand on our journey through the dark forest, walking toward the light.

Now, two years later, I finally understood the meaning of the dream: The boy in my dream was Little Shawn! I was stunned to think how incredible it was that God was showing me in my dreams what was to come, and also confirmed the very thing Ellie said I had to do: walk Little Shawn out of his darkness.

And so we began.

November 2009

Hi, Grandma,

I am sorry that is has taken me such a long time to write you. It will be difficult to explain all I've been going through and even still, you might not fully understand. I want to begin by telling you I love you very much and to thank you for the good memories I have from the times we spent together when I was a boy: The movie nights with chocolate popcorn, roasting marshmallows on the campfire next to your country home, the many songs you sang to me, the box of odds and ends you stored up to help feed my creative mind, and most of all, for occasionally letting me stay with you, which provided me a safe place to rest from the war of my childhood.

Thank you for telling me the last time I came for a visit that you were sorry for not rescuing me from the abuse, and that you never understood how bad it must have been for me.

I realized when I read the songs and poems from the little book you gave to me that you created when you were a girl—you are not a stranger to deep hurt, shame, and the feelings of being unloved. Thank you for all the times you told me you loved me. I so wanted and needed to be loved and I know that you really did.

Most of all, thank you for teaching me about Christ and His love for me. I know without a doubt that it was His hand that covered me through the darkest times. Where would we be without His love?

I recall telling Mom and Jed when I was in my first year of college that I forgave them. I worked so hard to put my childhood behind me. Although it was very painful for me, I did my best to try to build a relationship with them along with Jed's family. For years, I lived under the assumption that I'd dealt with my childhood and no longer lived under its bondage. I knew in my heart that I'd forgiven them but I never understood why I would *feel such a great darkness and depression come over me every time I would go to Ohio to visit.*

Going home would always trigger so many painful memories for me, but I did my best to block them out. I thought that's what I was supposed to do, if I'd really forgiven them. Instead, I was following the family tradition: <u>Don't think about it or talk about it; if it's in the past, act as though it never happened.</u>

Little did I know that the past I tried to lock away and forget was about to come rushing out of me like a tidal wave, forcing me to look at the pain of my childhood like never before.

It began when I started counseling at the church I was attending in south Houston with one of the pastors and a few other church Leaders. I came to understand that the deepest hurt and rejection I still struggled with stemmed from my relationship with Mom—something I never realized or fully understood. I had always associated most of my childhood trauma with Jed and his family.

Like most little boys, I always wanted to believe the best about my mom. I thought that I was supposed to protect her and stand by her, even though I never felt loved or wanted by her. She told me over and over that I didn't appreciate how good I had it, and that things were not as bad as I thought them to be. After a while, I guess I began to believe her. Believing that way has also helped me minimize the severity of the rejection and self-hatred I carried. Deep down, I believed that I was unlovable, stupid, ugly, and not good enough. My struggles with my sexuality only added to my heaping pile of shame.

At the end of March, following a series of events that triggered more childhood pain and trauma, I had a breakdown and had to be hospitalized. During my stay in the hospital, several childhood memories were triggered and I began to remember some horrific things that happened to me, things that my mind had completely blocked out because they were too painful. I was diagnosed with Chronic Post Traumatic Stress Disorder—the same disorder experienced by many soldiers when they return home from fighting in a war. My condition was so severe at first that I was also thought to be bipolar, which has since then been ruled out.

Shortly after, I began seeing a therapist weekly who specializes in treating adults who were abused as children. My therapist has estimated that the process I am walking through with her could take up to three years. The emotional work I'm doing is very difficult, but she says I am doing well.

I miss and love all of you greatly. Having to separate myself from you has been an incredibly difficult thing for me to do. Please know I have not done this to punish you in any way or to make you feel bad about what happened to me. I know in my heart that I have forgiven everyone involved. However, I am, for the first time in my life, having to keep myself in a safe place emotionally while I heal and grieve over what I lost and missed.

I am also learning what it is to accept myself as a Christian who is also gay, and not hate myself for it. I trust that the Lord knows my heart and I know that He loves me.

All my love,

Shawn

CHAPTER 19

———— ૪ ————

November 2009

Dear Mom,

I am sorry that it has been so long since you have heard from me. I honestly have not been emotionally able to contact you any sooner. The past eight months have been life-changing for me and I am learning to restructure my life in a way that is emotionally safe for me, which allows me to continue on the road to healing. As Grandma shares the details that I carefully presented in her letter, I hope you will be able to see that none of this has been pre-planned or dramatized in any way, but is simply the reality of what I'm walking through. I am forging a new path each day by faith with the One who created me. Many times, I feel as though I won't survive, but I have, and I am still surviving. The Lord is merciful!

I want you to know how thankful I am for some of the happier memories we were able to create together as I became an adult. I saw you change in amazing ways and I do believe that you grew to love me in the best way you could.

However, if I am really gut-level honest from the deepest part of me, I must confess that the good times often have been overshadowed by the immense black hole that still remains from my lost childhood. I say none of this to hurt you or to point the finger of blame or judgment.

I will not claim, nor would I ever try to suggest that I know everything about the pain and suffering you have endured in your own personal life. I do believe that it is far more than you have ever disclosed to me.

I understand that too often, we find ourselves on a vicious roller-coaster ride made up of what we've had handed to us, without our consent, inherited from generations before us. All I know, Mom, is that I want to get off the ride. The little boy in me that was so hurt doesn't want to play in that game any longer. He wants to be whole and healthy and to be able to live a happy and fulfilling life without the debilitating shame and self-hate.

You have told me in times past that you could not go on this journey with me because it was too painful for you. You stated that you did not want to remember. I respect that, and I force nothing on you. I only hope that you can also respect this new path that I have chosen and am determined to walk on, even though it may seem foreign and uncomfortable for you.

Please never forget that I love you, Mom. When I said I forgave you years ago, I did, and that has never changed. You are a beautiful woman who has been created in the Father's image and His love for you is as endless as the stars in the sky.

All my love,

Shawn

I wish I could say the responses I received back from the letters I wrote to my mother and grandmother were full of acceptance and unconditional love, but unfortunately, they were not. When Grandma wrote me back, she did again acknowledge the pain of my childhood, telling me how sorry she was for any part she played. But all the kind things she wrote grew dim as she began to preach that the life I was living would lead me to hell. Out of all the things I poured out to her in my letter, it felt as though the part she focused on the most was my admission, "*I am also learning what it is to accept myself as a Christian who is also gay.*" Even though this might not have been true, it came across that way.

It was a part of Grandma that even after all these years still surprised me. Because she was so incredibly sweet, I was never prepared for the times she would bluntly put me down. Like the time when I was in high school, planning for a career on Broadway, when Grandma said to me, "Shawn, you should only be using your gifts for the Lord. He's gonna knock you off this pedestal you've put yourself on!"

It was as though the behavior didn't even fit with who I knew her to be; however, with the deep emotional work I was doing in therapy, I was able to see what it was all about. It most likely came from her own shame that she carried. People who are full of shame in turn shame others. It's a defense mechanism that was developed to avoid seeing inside. It had become such a part of her response system that she probably didn't even realize she did it.

Although I overlooked Grandma's first letter of reply containing her religious need to tell me I was going to hell, I was no longer willing to accept this behavior from her after she refused to stop in her second and third letters.

The last time I'd had contact with Mom before I wrote her and Grandma the letters was a few days after I left the hospital. I was still struggling from the PTSD, and some of the things I said probably didn't make much sense. I'm sure I didn't sound like myself.

I couldn't seem to help myself for sharing with her some of the memories that came up for me in the hospital, and I probably wasn't too good at softening things as I usually did. I could hear in her voice that she sounded hurt when she said, Shawn "Why would you tell me things like that? I can't believe that you would hurt me like this."

But it didn't take long before her hurt turned to anger, and she defensively snapped at me, saying, "Who do you think you are, buster?! I can't believe that you would make up things like this!"

I knew that voice: It was the same voice that frightened me as a child, and it still did. In my emotionally fragile state, I said, "Mom, I just wanted to tell you what was going on, but I can't talk to you anymore now. I gotta go." And I hung up.

My therapist encouraged me to wait until I was in a better place emotionally before I reached out to them again, and it was another eight months, around Thanksgiving, when I eventually sent them and my sister Hailey the letters.

The only response I received from the letter I wrote to Mom were a few words written in my birthday card that she sent me two months later: "Shawn, I have no idea where you're coming up with all this stuff, but you were definitely right when you said don't know what I've been through!" There was absolutely no mention of any concern for my welfare.

Before I wrote the letters, I waited until I felt that I could accept any response that might come back. I told myself that my only purpose for writing them was to deliver the message, realizing that I had no control over how either recipient would respond. Nonetheless, to say their responses didn't hurt would not be human.

For Christmas, I sent a card and a family gift, but for the first time since adulthood, I didn't call Mom and Grandma. Grandma sent me a Christmas card with another note, telling me the Lord was coming back soon and I'd better get ready.

My sister Hailey eventually called me a month later and left me a sweet phone message asking me to call her back, but when I spoke with her, I was quickly reminded that she was Jed's daughter as she lit into me like a bully on the rampage.

She told me what a horrible person I was for not calling Mom, and that everyone knew I was fabricating the stories of my childhood. Hailey said Mom thought I was probably mentally ill and "crazy in the head" just like the rest of my dad's family. I reminded Hailey that I am six years older than she, and that my experience of our family differs vastly from hers. Still, it was obvious to me that my sister was compartmentalizing many things as well.

I also realized that Hailey wasn't well mentally or emotionally, just like her dad. She had never been very stable—a fact I had recognized for some time, thinking she might be bipolar. I cried many times in prayer asking God to heal her. There were also probably times I prayed for her just out of the guilt I carried. I never understood why I didn't seem to see God's hand of mercy on my little sister as I did on myself. It always perplexed me, and I grieved over it.

The ironic part of Mom's assessment of my and my father's mental illness was her inability to see that very thing right in front of her, with

Jed and his family. When Ellie told me that Jed and my dad were psychopathic, I went home and researched it. I couldn't believe how accurately the research described both of them, and how many of the traits and characteristics were spot on, especially for Jed (perhaps more obvious to me because I spent a lot more time with him growing up).

Ellie encouraged me to set new boundaries with my family (something that had always been hard for me) in a way I'd never done before, and cut off all contact. The thought of doing that terrified me, since it went against everything that had been drilled into my head since I was a child—such as all that "blood is thicker than water" rationalization.

I also struggled with what I believed about forgiveness and honoring my mother. Again, God knew exactly what I needed when He gave me Ellie. She, too, knew the scriptures, and quoted one of them to me one afternoon before she said, "Shawn, forgiveness doesn't always mean restored relationship."

By the look on my face, she could tell that I was troubled. Ellie asked, "When you were a pastor, would you have a counseled a woman who was being abused by her husband to stay with him and take it?"

"Absolutely not," I responded assuredly.

"Then why would God want you to stay in a relationship with your abusive family who is hurting you?"

I paused for a minute, as the truth of what she was saying sank deeper into my mind. I'd never really thought about it in those terms because of the way I'd minimized and hidden away so much. I also never processed that my family's unwillingness to accept me for who I am was continuing to hurt me. Every time they said they would never accept me as gay, they communicated to me all over again that I wasn't enough.

Ellie said it was understandable why boundaries were so hard for me with my family, because they had crossed every single one of mine when I was a child. I was taught that boundaries didn't matter. Now it was time for me to teach Little Shawn what healthy boundaries look like and how important they are. Ellie explained to me that when new boundaries are set with people who have none, they will get angry, manipulate, and push back. They will do whatever they feel is necessary to try to force me drop my boundaries.

It took me about two years before I stopped feeling bad for setting my boundaries and to stop grieving the separation from my family; Mothers Day and Christmas were always the worst. It was one of the hardest things I've ever done emotionally, but it gave me the space I needed to actively begin applying the principles I was learning in therapy, and to heal. Surprisingly, the longer I was removed from my families' toxicity, the clearer my understanding became.

Not long after I ceased communication, I also joined a twelve-step program and began working on addiction recovery. Although Ellie had brought up the idea to me several times, it took me a while before I finally responded. The thought of attending weekly meetings with strangers and sharing openly about my hidden compartments terrified me.

The newly added layer of shame produced from my addiction only tightened its grip on me; it's why I believe it took such considerable effort to pry me from its unmerciful imprisonment. Knowing I had been a pastor, one who had counseled others through their dark times of pain and hopelessness, made it even more unbearable for me. I guess I felt that more than anyone, I should have known better.

I had grown up in a home with addicts; my stepfather was a drug dealer. I knew full well the destructive powers of drugs and alcohol. This is why I wanted nothing to do with any of those when I was growing up.

I remember even carrying a hidden disdain for those who drank excessively and used drugs. I tried my best to not show this when others came to me for help with their addictions during my years in the ministry. However, deep down, I didn't get it. I was so self-righteous with my inner judgments and assessments as to what they should do; I looked at addiction as nothing more than a lack of discipline or a weakness. Was I ever wrong! I was only transferring my own internal blame and pain onto these precious hearts that were so courageous in their pursuit of freedom.

The people in the program taught me that addiction is a disease of the brain which produces a mental obsession that cannot be restrained easily. I was beginning to see that I was powerless to help myself and couldn't do it on my own. At first, that was a difficult admission, since I'd survived my childhood and still accomplished so many things. I had always believed I could do all things with Christ's help. But the Scripture also teaches us to confess our faults to others, so that we may be healed—and that has always been a tough one for me. I was really good at confessing things to God, but I didn't want anyone else to know about it. I put myself under so much pressure for so long, caring about what others thought.

The time had come for me to humble myself, come out of my isolation, and realize how desperately I needed others if I were to stay sober. The road was difficult, but I was determined to not give up.

I've lived most of my life with one thought in the past and the next in the future, but my new friends in my weekly support group were helping me see the importance of staying focused on what's in front of me—one day at a time.

My eyes were continuously being opened to a whole new world like never before, and I had a new determination to do whatever it took to get better. After Ellie and I finished our three years of working together, I began a seeing another therapist who specialized in addiction as well as childhood trauma. Her area of specialty sounded like the perfect combination for me.

I couldn't imagine anybody taking Ellie's place—until I met Iris. If the relationship I had with Ellie could be described as that of a grandmother and grandson, the relationship I shared with Iris would definitely be best friends.

Iris was very professional and we never saw each other outside of our weekly sessions, but we had a rare connection. She really "got" me. And, just as best friends often do, she was also able to read me when something was off, and didn't let me get away with much. God's mercy was again providing me just what I needed.

Not long after I began working with Iris, she seemed to be completely fascinated one day when I described to her how I'd gotten myself up, dressed, and walked down to the little white church alone when I was seven years old. To her, this had required an unusual amount of resilience; to me, it was just survival.

Iris said that instead of developing the attachment most children have with their parents when they're very young, I had that with the church. This is why, she believed, that I struggled off and on after I came out of the closet and kept running back to the church for comfort and acceptance: I longed and needed to hear from my attachment figure that I was going to be okay. The worst part about this dysfunctional cycle was that my attachment figure was never going to tell me I was okay if I was gay; the acceptance part was always going to be conditional. On the other hand, Iris also told me with certainty that the vision I'd had of Jesus when I was a little boy saved my mind.

Later that day, I couldn't stop thinking about all that Iris had said to me, as I began to question: Was my vision real? Did I really see Jesus? Did I see heaven? Or was it the way my strong young intellect had subconsciously incorporated all the things I was being taught at the little church to steady my emotions and preserve my traumatized mind? The vision was undoubtedly so crucial to my survival because it instilled within me a sense of importance which I so desperately needed. It created within me a belief that I mattered and that my life had purpose.

With all my heart, I do believe in God and His ability to communicate to us, just like He had done several times in my dreams. However, to me, it is completely irrelevant as to why and how I had the vision; only that I most assuredly did have it.

The next time I went into Iris's office, I was completely high strung, stressed out over a workshop I was writing and scheduled to facilitate at a teaching hospital two weeks later.

Recognizing my anxiety, Iris said, "Shawn, you have to learn how to relax. The more stressed out you get, the more you're going to struggle."

Upset, feeling like she just wasn't getting where I was coming from, I defensively snapped at her and said, "You don't understand, this is really important! There will be around fifty doctors there. I have to knock this out of the park!"

Iris wasn't buying that. "Why do you have to knock it out of the park?" she asked calmly.

When I didn't respond, Iris smiled and added, "Knocking it out of the park is good if you mean going in and relaxing and doing the best you can for now. But knocking it out of the park is *not good* if you mean it has to be perfect."

I felt more frustrated in my therapy session with Iris that day than I'd felt for a while, but I knew she was right. I had struggled with perfectionism all my life. Feeling as if I weren't enough drove me to try to make up for it with the things I did, although in my mind it was an impossible task, because nothing I did was ever good enough. I'm sure it's probably why I completely bombed an assessment that Iris gave me on self-compassion. She said I basically had none, which explains why I beat myself up whenever I made a mistake. My self-talk had been absolutely brutal for as long as I could remember.

The next time I met with Iris after she returned from vacation, she asked me how the workshop had gone and I told her, "Honestly, it didn't go so well."

As she sat there looking at me with suspicion, I added, "Listen, I understand what you were talking about the last time about perfectionism, and I agree I have to keep working on that. However, this didn't go well because of something else."

Leaning forward, I continued, "All my life, I have struggled greatly when I feel intimidated; it's as though my mind goes blank and I completely lose my words. It's been so frustrating for me! I continuously hear others tell me how well-spoken I am, and that I have a gift for public speaking, so I know the gifting is there, but when this thing happens that I am telling you about, I feel like a complete babbling fool. It's been such a love-hate relationship I've had with public speaking because when I'm on, I absolutely love it, and wouldn't want to be anywhere else. But when I'm not on, it's bad, and I just want to crawl under a table and hide. What's even more confusing is it just doesn't happen when I'm in front of an audience: There have been countless times when the same thing happens in front of just one person."

Iris said, "Shawn, I think that the perfectionism and what you're talking about is all interconnected; it all has to do with the ability to relax." At that, she went over to her desk and pulled out a four-by-five card. Handing the card to me, she asked, "Why don't you take a moment to read this and tell me what you think?"

After I read the words of the Chinese proverb she had written on the card, I froze. It was as though the words had been written specifically for me. They perfectly described what I've always felt inside, but never fully understood:

"Tension is who you think you should be. Relaxation is who you are."

Slowly lifting my head from staring at the card, I said, "It's scary how much I relate to these words. Relaxing is something I've never been able to do around others. When I was little, I was constantly measuring the temperature of every environment, every conversation, and every action to see if it felt safe. If it began to turn cold, I would quickly search for the exit. Even after all these years, I still catch myself doing it more times than I would like to admit. Just like the perfectionism, it's absolutely exhausting!"

Iris explained to me it had everything to do with the altered brain chemistry Ellie had taught me about from the all the childhood trauma. I had been living life in a state of hyper-vigilance, never fully feeling that I could relax, always waiting for the trauma to occur.

Iris said what I described about my mind blanking out and losing my words was a typical fight-or-flight response in the brain. When that happens, I'm no longer operating out of the front part of my brain, where my intelligence and gifts live, but I'm in the back part of the brain, which is all about survival. According to Iris, once I'm in the back part of the brain, it completely takes over and shuts off the front. She said because my brain chemistry baseline for anxiety is already set high, I get there much more quickly than most people do.

As I listened to all that she was saying, so many things began to make sense: Why my voice professor in college my freshman year kept telling me how unusually tense I was, and I needed to relax more if I were ever going to sing properly; why a chiropractor who treated me for a period of time continued to say to me, "You carry so much tension in your back. You have to learn how to release it if you're going get better." And all the frustrated times throughout my life driving in the car, that my mind went blank and I got lost, sometimes for hours. I was always so embarrassed and humiliated that I never told anyone just how bad it was.

After I related all this to Iris, she kindly said, "Shawn, once again, this is just another confirmation of how much resilience you have. It also takes a high level of intellect and emotional intelligence to be able to maneuver around something like this and to accomplish all the things you have. I really hope you understand that."

When she said that, my entire being took in a big breath and sighed out enormous relief. "All these years, I thought it was just me," I said in amazement. I felt so emotional that it was difficult to hold back the tears.

All this time, I had put myself down for a stupid side-effect of my abusive childhood. If I had only known. It's as though I had been abusing Little Shawn all over again, and for what? Something I had no control over.

Still numb from this enlightenment, I asked Iris, "Is there anything I can do to change this?"

"Actually, there is," she said with a reassuring smile. "There are some pre-recorded breathing and muscle relaxation exercises that have been strategically designed by a well-known college of medicine that you can listen to. They have been proven to rewire the brain chemistry and reset your baseline of serenity. If you're willing to listen to these multiple times a week, over time you will feel much more relaxed and it will take it a much greater amount of stress and anxiety to trigger you into *flight or fight* than it does now. It will help you to remain in the front part of your brain, and stay connected with what's in front of you."

Iris's plan worked, and everyone who knew me well saw the difference.

By the time I finished my three-and-a-half-year wellness journey with Iris, I felt entirely different in my own skin. My life had transformed in so many ways that I felt like I'd been given a second chance to live.

How incongruous that the healing I'd needed and sought for such a long time was waiting for me all along in entities deemed harmful by many in Christendom: psychotherapy, deep breathing and relaxation exercises, and a twelve-step program. Perhaps it's just another way of God confirming for me that we don't, nor will we ever in this lifetime, have Him all figured out.

Sitting alongside the clergy in front of the packed sanctuary, I felt excited but calm. The deep-breathing exercises I'd done in the pastor's office a few minutes earlier were working. As the Sunday-morning worship service began, I continued to remind myself to breathe and relax. I had stood in front of church congregations hundreds of times, but it had never felt like this before. All the other times, I was filled with anxiety, buried under shame, and feeling like an imposter. But this time, I felt peace—the brand of peace that comes only from being open and honest.

When the opening-worship music ended and the pastor walked up to the lectern to make the announcements and introduce me as the guest speaker, I suddenly caught the sparkling blue eyes of my handsome coffee-shop encounter sitting among the crowd. We had met unexpectedly one afternoon when I stopped for a coffee after a speaking engagement. Our connection was instantaneous, and the potential for something substantial felt strong.

As I heard the Pastor call my name and I began walking forward, I remembered something an old friend had said to me many times: "The day you finally get hold of what's inside you and realize all you're capable of, is the day you're gonna fly!"

I had my wings, and I was already ten feet off the ground.

Epilogue

As I FACED the empty lot on Chester Street where my house and the rose bush had once been, I could still see the gray-and-white shingled structure with my bedroom window on the second floor—the window that had given me an imaginary view of a different life. As the vision of my memory faded, I smiled at the realization of how symbolic it was that the old house—a representation of my childhood suffering, along with the thorny rose bush—was gone.

Wanting to take full advantage of this special moment, I wondered, *"What do you feel, Shawn?"*

I feel relieved, at peace. I no longer feel like running and hiding from the shame of my life as I did for so many years. Everything has changed. Most important, *I have changed!* My endless hours of prayer, deep emotional work, and years of therapy have replanted me in a much better place. The thorns of Chester Street that were embedded deeply in my heart have withered into the ground and become the fertilizer for the man I am today. For that, I am forever grateful.

Forgiveness is the healing ointment to the aching wounds of disappointment; the key that unlocks the prison door of anger. Forgiveness is the medicine that cleanses the soul from the poisonous toxicity of bitterness and resentment. We must choose to forgive if we are to truly live.

Shawn

Shawn at age 7

Acknowledgements

MY DEEPEST GRATITUDE goes to my heavenly Father; Lee Willis; Jeanne Higgs; Dr. Shannon Schrader; my writing mentor and editor Van English; Dr. Pedro Diaz-Marchan; Ann Taylor; Rev. Troy Plummer Treash; David McGurk; Erin Magana; Dr. Richard Fish; Anna Hathaway McKee; and last but definitely not least, my blue-eyed coffee shop encounter, Mike Martin.

About the Author

—— ❦ ——

SHAWN ALEX NEMETH was born in Marion, Ohio, in 1969, where he lived until he graduated from high school. He attended Ohio University as a vocal-performance major and Greenville College in Illinois, studying contemporary Christian music. Shawn later earned his bachelor's degree in theology and was ordained into the ministry; he served two churches in Illinois and one in California as a pastor, worship leader, and missions director. In 1997, Shawn joined the faculty at Christ for the Nations Institute in Dallas, Texas, as the Director of *Living Praise*, traveling and ministering extensively throughout the United States and abroad.

A gifted speaker, coach, and inspirational leader, Shawn helps people develop insight and shares tools and techniques that allow them to dramatically change their lives. Owner and proprietor of both a successful wellness coaching practice and a fitness coaching business, he emphatically believes and serves as a model to illustrate that people can—with the right amounts of faith, resilience, courage, and encouragement—become their very best selves.

Shawn is professionally certified by the Life Coach Institute of Orange County, the Fowler International Academy of Professional Coaching, and the International Sports Sciences Association. He is founder and President of the Chester Street Foundation, a nonprofit organization that seeks, secures, and distributes funding for professional services to children who are abused, bullied, neglected, or otherwise compromised.

He currently lives in Houston with his partner of seven years, Mike. Together, they enjoy movies, traveling, hiking in the Texas Hill Country, and relaxing jaunts to Galveston Island.

——⟆

To engage Shawn as a speaker for your event,
please visit www.shawnalexnemeth.com

CHESTER STREET
FOUNDATION

HEALING HEARTS AND MINDS

Mission

- Our mission is to heal the hearts and minds of abused children through recovery, research, and education.

Purposes   Core Values

- Charitable   - Compassion
- Scientific   - Integrity
- Educational   - Innovation

www.chesterstreetfoundation.org

Proceeds from the sale of this book will benefit
the Chester Street Foundation.